# The Ultimate
# MUSHROOM BOOK

# The Ultimate
# MUSHROOM BOOK

The complete guide to identifying, picking and using mushrooms –
a photographic A – Z of types and 100 original recipes

## Peter Jordan & Steven Wheeler

### Consultant: Geoffrey Kibby

HERMES
HOUSE

This edition published in 1998 by Hermes House
27 West 20th Street, New York, NY 10011

HERMES HOUSE books are available for bulk purchase for sales
promotion and for premium use. For details, write or call the sales
director, Hermes House, 27 West 20th Street, New York, NY 10011;
(800) 354-9657

© Anness Publishing Limited 1995

Hermes House is an imprint of
Anness Publishing Inc.

ISBN 1-84038-132-9

*Publisher* Joanna Lorenz
*Project editor* Clare Nicholson
*Indexer* Alex Corrin
*Designer* Michael Morey
*Illustrator* Adam Abel
*Photography for field guide* Peter Henley
*Photography for cookbook* James Duncan

Typeset by MC Typeset Ltd, England

Printed and bound in China

1 3 5 7 9 10 8 6 4 2

# CONTENTS

# Introduction

# FOREWORD

I was introduced to wild mushrooms by my grandfather who was a farmer in Norfolk, England. From the age of four I would go out in the fields with him to collect not only what he described as field mushrooms, but also some weird and wonderful looking mushrooms which I thought were poisonous – they certainly looked menacing to a child. However, he taught me one very good lesson: as long as you can identify absolutely accurately what you are picking you will be safe. From these early beginnings developed a lifetime's interest in mushrooms.

The excitement of walking along a woodland path in the autumn, and finding in front of you two or three perfectly formed ceps is wonderful. During fifty years as a mushroom hunter, I have graduated from the relatively common horse and field mushrooms to the more exotic chanterelles and ceps. I am still excited when I find the first morels of the spring, or the year's first patch of chanterelles hidden in the leaf mold; of course, the more elusive the mushroom, like the horn of plenty or the winter chanterelle, the greater the excitement. Imagine the ultimate triumph of finding your first giant puffball – it's head actually bigger than your own! But, as well as providing excitement and good eating, mushrooms can be dangerous; correct identification is the key to successful mushroom collecting.

The fruits, nuts and mushrooms of autumn are obvious and most are easy to spot. But have you ever realized that the winter, spring and summer can be as productive – at least as far as mushrooms are concerned? Mushrooms are one of the few wild treasures available nearly all the year round. Even on a crisp winter's day you can find a bouquet of silver-gray oyster mushrooms or the wonderful velvet shank growing out of a tree stump and it is so much more satisfying to pick them like this than from a supermarket shelf. Because, of course, the excitement of finding the mushrooms is closely followed by the satisfaction of cooking them within hours if not minutes of their harvest.

Identifying mushrooms, utterly essential though it is, can be frustrating if you have to wade through hundreds of illustrations, many of which look the same. This book is designed to make that task easier. It illustrates the best of the edible mushrooms, and so will help you pick your way wisely through the year's mushrooms, alerting you not only to a season's treasures, but also to the poisonous lookalikes and really deadly fungi that all too often grow alongside innocent and delicious mushrooms. The section that deals with the poisonous species will help identification and give the faint-hearted confidence to take their finds back to the kitchen. But do follow the advice given in this guide carefully. If clear identification is not possible from this book, consult others – the bibliography lists some of the best. And remember that the best advice of all is: if in doubt do not collect a mushroom and never, ever, eat anything you cannot identify with certainty.

*Peter Jordan*

# WHAT ARE MUSHROOMS?

The terms mushrooms, toadstools and fungi (singular fungus) are often used loosely and interchangeably. However, this can be misleading.

The fungi are a very large group of organisms and include moulds, yeasts, mushrooms and toadstools. None of these organisms contain the green pigment chlorophyll, so they cannot make their own food by the process known as photosynthesis. So, although you may encounter some mushrooms with a distinctly greenish tinge, none are green in the way that a tree or a flowering plant is.

Mushrooms are usually defined as the edible, spore-producing bodies of some fungi. In contrast, the term toadstool is commonly applied to the spore-producing bodies of those fungi that are not only inedible but may also be highly dangerous. From this you will realize that while the terms fungus and fungi have a very precise scientific meaning, mushroom and toadstool do not. In this book mushroom is used whether, or not, the fruit body of that particular fungus is edible. It is used to cover a large number of different types of fungi such as mushrooms, boletes, bracket fungi, puff balls and cap fungi.

**Ascomycetes**

*The cup fungi circle shows details of the spore-bearing surface.*

**Basidiomycetes**

*The gilled mushroom circle shows the enlargement of the gill edge.*

Tuber aestivum, *the summer truffle, an example of an ascomycete fungus.*

The fungi in this book divide into two main groups: the Ascomycetes and the Basidiomycetes. The Ascomycetes produce spores that are spread by the wind. Among this group are many of the cup fungi, including the common morel and *Gyromitra esculenta*. Because the wind spreads the spore of many of these mushrooms, it is worth remembering when you find some morels, for example, to check downwind and you will almost certainly find some more.

The second group, and by far the largest as far as the collector is concerned, is the Basidiomycetes, which includes the large and well-known Agaric and Boletus families. These two families, in fact, form sub-divisions within the group.

A mushroom of the Agaric type is illustrated here with the various parts clearly identified. This is a gilled mushroom and sometimes grows from an egg-shaped volval bag. Care must be taken when dealing with any mushroom that grows from a volval bag, because this is how the *Amanitas*, the most deadly of all mushroom species, grow.

### Parts of the Agaric-type fungi

*The universal veil encloses the whole mushroom and the partial veil covers the gills. As the mushroom grows the universal veil ruptures to leave a volva and fragments on the cap, and the partial veil ruptures to leave a ring on the stem.*

### Parts of the Boletus-type fungi

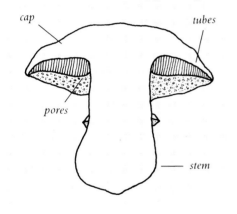

A second sub-division is the Boletes. Instead of having gills, mushrooms in this group have tubes and pores which vary widely in colour. Boletes, like Agarics, are fleshy and decay readily. This separates them from the Polypores. It is important to note their colour because this can be a clear indicator of the mushrooms you have found. The cep is the best-known member of this group.

A third group of fungi illustrated in this book is Aphyllophorales. This group includes the polypores and chanterelles and a number of other mushrooms that have irregular shapes. A number of fungi fall into this group, for example, the hedgehog fungus, which, instead of gills, has tiny spines from which it gets its name. Another member of the group is the cauliflower fungus. It may look odd, but it is a wonderful find from a culinary point of view. Other unusual types are the beefsteak fungus and the sulphur polypore or chicken of the woods. Both are excellent for cooking as well as being quite spectacular when you encounter them in the wild.

*Examples of the two types of fungi which form sub-divisions of the Basidiomycetes. The horse mushroom (above) and the cep (right).*

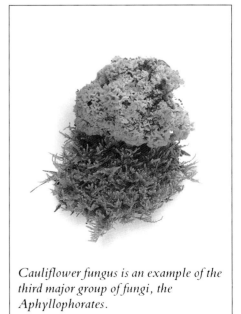

*Cauliflower fungus is an example of the third major group of fungi, the Aphyllophorates.*

# THE DIFFERENT PARTS OF MUSHROOMS

When you start collecting wild mushrooms it is important to consider carefully what it is that you are collecting. The mushroom itself can be divided into various parts. From both the collecting and culinary points of view the cap of the fruit body is the most important part. The shape, size and color of the cap can show tremendous variation within a species, which is one of the reasons why mushrooms are so difficult to identify accurately. It is also important to note whether the cap has gills or pores, what the colors of these are and whether they are crowded or open.

Stems can also vary considerably and they, too, can often be an important indicator of precisely which mushroom you have discovered. Does the stem have a veil or not? The base of the stem is a vital means of identification, particularly if you have any doubts about the specimens you have found. If you are not sure what it is, carefully dig out the mushroom so that you can see the base of the stem. If there is any sign of a volval cup have nothing more to do with the mushroom. Incidentally, whatever the mushroom that you are digging up proves to be, be careful not to do too much damage to the mycelial threads that connect it to the rest of the underground part of the fungus.

The color of the mushroom's flesh is another important means of identification. Not only should you look at the whole mushroom, you should also cut it through in cross-section. Some important details, such as whether the stem is hollow, can of course, only be seen in cross-section. In some species the stems change color quite dramatically when they are cut. Take note of any such changes, because they can be a reliable identification feature in certain types of mushroom.

Spore prints are also a good means of identifying mushrooms and are very easy to do. Take a cap of a mature specimen of a mushroom and place it on black and white paper on top of a container. Cover with a glass or shallow bowl. Then let sit for a few hours to a day so the mushroom sheds all its spores and you will have a very clear spore print. If you do not know what color the spore will be, put down a piece of black paper and overlay part of it with white paper. Then place the cap so that it is half on the black paper and half on the white.

**Examples of different shapes of stems**

**LEFT** *To take a spore print you will need a mature specimen, white, or black and white paper and a container to place it on.*

**LEFT BELOW** *Leave the mushroom in a warm place for a few hours to one day.*

**LEFT BOTTOM** *Do not use just black paper because it will not show up if the spore print is a dark color.*

**BELOW** *Taking a spore print is a very reliable way of making an accurate identification.*

# WHERE TO COLLECT MUSHROOMS

Always take care when you are out mushroom collecting that you do not trespass. Always get the permission of the landowner before you go on to any land that is not open to the public. When you are mushroom collecting be careful of the surrounding countryside and its animals, otherwise not only will you soon get a bad reputation, but you will give other collectors a similar reputation whether they deserve it or not.

Most people limit their mushroom hunting to meadows, but these have suffered from being over enriched with nitrates, which have denuded many previously good mushroom-hunting territories. If you want to find meadowland mushrooms it is best to examine those meadows and marshes that have been treated with natural organic fertilizers and not nitrates. But why restrict yourself to meadowland species when eighty per cent of fungi grow in association

with trees? Woods, forests and copses are the places where you should really be looking for mushrooms, but only, of course, once you have established you will not be trespassing.

Established woods and forests containing a wide variety of species provide the very best places for mushroom collecting and it is in such areas that the vast majority of species are to be found. Many of these fungi have a symbiotic relationship with trees and their roots, with some fungi growing only with a particular species of tree, while other fungi can be found in association with a number of different trees. For example, many boletes grow only with one type of tree such as the species of *Suillus* which only grow with conifers, or the species of *Leccinum* which are very specific: *Leccinum versipelle* grows with birch and *L. aurantiacum* with aspen. Chanterelles on the other hand can effectively grow with birch,

pine, oaks or even beech trees.

Soil type is also important. Although many trees grow on a variety of soils, you will find that some fungi will only grow with a particular tree on a particular soil, rather than across the whole range of soils on which the tree grows. For example the bay boletus grows under beech trees or under conifers on acid soils, and the panther cap grows under beech trees on chalk.

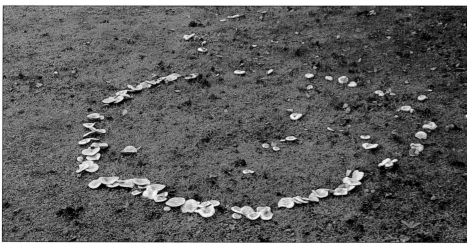

**ABOVE** *The early morning is prime mushroom hunting time.*

**OPPOSITE** *Do not restrict your mushroom hunting to meadows and woodlands: marshes and heathland can be surprisingly productive too.*

**LEFT** *Many mushrooms grow in rings, some of which reach several metres wide.*

# WHEN TO COLLECT MUSHROOMS

Most people associate mushrooms with the autumn, but, in fact, they grow throughout the year.

The spring brings morels and the St George's mushroom *Calocybe gambosa*. The fairy ring mushroom, *Marasmius oreades*, also appears quite early in the year. The first of the summer mushrooms is usually the field mushroom, *Agaricus campestris*. Another mushroom to appear fairly early in summer is the chicken of the woods, *Laetiporus sulphureus*, indeed it often catches collectors unawares with its early appearance. When, or indeed if, there is a spell of hot weather, there is usually little to be found, but these conditions are, nevertheless, important, because they help the mushrooms' underground mycelial threads to mature before the autumn's great burst of growth. If the weather is mild, the autumn can extend into early winter. The first touches of frost may herald the com-

ing of winter, but they can often bring exciting finds of both the brick cap, *Naemataloma sublateritium*, and the blewit, *Lepista nuda*. Both these species will continue until the weather turns quite frosty.

When winter takes hold, most

people give up and just look forward to the next mushroom season. But don't be fooled: on mild winter days in more temperate zones, go out searching and you will be surprised at what you find. Oyster mushrooms, *Pleurotus ostreatus*, will continue to grow almost right through the winter, together with the tree ear, *Auricularia auricula*, and the velvet shank, *Flammulina velutipes*. Finding these can make a cold winter walk tremendously exciting, and shows that even in the depth of winter you can enjoy a dish with ingredients freshly picked from fields and woods.

The mushroom collector's year never ends and even when you're not actually hunting, always be on the lookout for new spots. Use winter walks to examine pastures and woodlands that you have not been to before, to see if they give any clues as to what they are likely to produce when spring comes again.

It may seem surprising, but time of day is most important to the mushroom collector. This is because mushrooms grow almost exclusively during the hours of darkness. As a result, the best specimens are picked when they are fresh in the early morning before the rising temperature of the day has brought out the flies to lay their eggs, so giving rise to insect infestation, or the animals of the woods and fields have had their pickings of the overnight growth, which can be quite amazing in its quantity.

It is also worth revisiting a place you have picked after two or three days, because the mushrooms will usually have grown back. Ceps are known to grow back to a weight of 1¾ lb within two or three days of the first growth having been picked – an enormous rate of growth by any standard.

It is useful to keep a diary of what you find, when and where you found it, and what the climatic conditions were, as this will give you a key to subsequent seasons and help you develop a knowledge and understanding of your local area. Noting climatic conditions is also interesting as well as useful. Good fungal growth needs periods of damp, but also periods of dry and cold, as the mycelial threads seem to benefit from a degree of stratification which, in turn, gives rise to better fruiting, and thus to better collecting.

**OPPOSITE ABOVE** *Chicken of the woods grows from late spring to early autumn.*

**OPPOSITE BELOW** *Oyster mushrooms continue to grow through the winter.*

**ABOVE** *The poisonous* Clitocybe rivulosa *appears in summer and autumn.*

**LEFT** *Blewits.*

# HOW TO COLLECT MUSHROOMS

Very little equipment is needed for mushroom collecting. Tough outdoor clothes and a strong pair of boots are essential and you should make sure that your jacket or parka has a pocket large enough to carry a small field guide. It is not an exaggeration: some mushrooms are just too dangerous to take home. You may find a wide-brimmed hat useful to wear in the autumn, as the days shorten and the sun is low. It is easier to spot those interesting little humps and bumps that could well prove to be an exciting find if you are not having to shade your eyes with your hand all the time.

One or two baskets are, of course, essential. They should be light, easy to carry and not too open in weave. A sharp knife and brush are also important, the knife to cut the mushroom's stem through cleanly and the brush to remove obvious dirt and debris such as pine needles and leaf mold. Cleaning your specimens as you pick them will mean there is less to do when you get home. Several plastic bags or disposable gloves are also essential items to take with

**OPPOSITE**
*Results of a
successful
morning's
mushroom
collecting.*

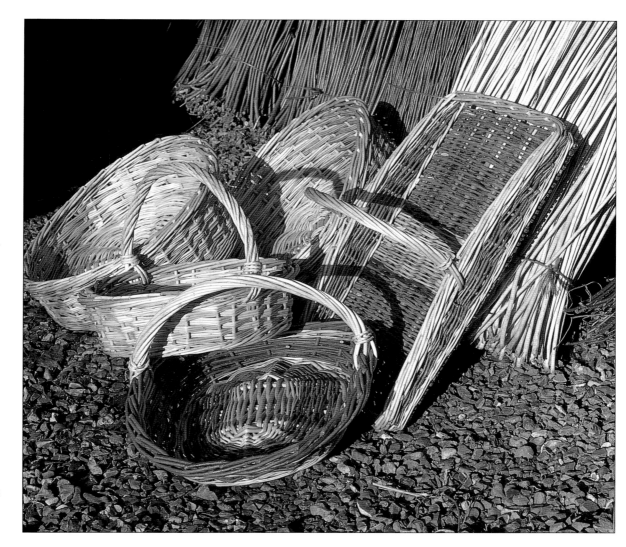

**RIGHT** *A selection
of handmade
baskets.*

you. You can put these over your hands when handling any specimens about which you are doubtful. Don't forget to throw them away after you have used them. A package of tissues or a cloth will also be useful as your hands can get quite dirty. You will also need them to clean your knife, as you should clean it each time you use it.

The final item of equipment is a good strong stick. You can use it to part ferns and undergrowth to see if any mushrooms are hidden there. It will be handy to turn over any specimens you may not wish to touch, as well as being useful as a tool to dig out specimens so that you can check if they have volval cups or not.

When you find a specimen that you can identify with certainty and want to collect, it is best to cut

**BELOW** *A good knife is an essential part of any mushroom collector's equipment. Two of the knives here double as a brush as well.*

through its stem rather than dig it up. While it is possible to use the stems of mushrooms such as ceps and chanterelles, there is a danger of disturbing the mycelial threads if the entire mushroom is removed from the ground. The only possible exception to this rule is if you are confronted by what you think may be a poisonous mushroom. Then dig it up with your stick, being careful not to damage it. If there is anything that looks even remotely like a volval cup at the base of the stem, leave the whole specimen well alone.

Having cut through the mushroom's stem, wipe or brush clean the mushroom before putting it in your basket. As the basket starts to fill up, a layer of fern fronds will prevent the bottom mushrooms from becoming damaged.

# STORING MUSHROOMS

There are certain times of the year when mushrooms grow in great profusion. It is important, therefore, to find ways to preserve this abundance for those times when few mushrooms grow. Preserving food is as old as time itself and long before refrigerators, salting and drying were used as methods of preservation. There are many different ways to store mushrooms and some species are more suited to a certain type of preservation than others. Informa-

laying them on cheesecloth trays in the sun can be quite sufficient. In cooler, less sunny regions, mushrooms can be dried on open trays in a warm stove, and on window sills. It is important to remember that the mushrooms must be dried thoroughly, which may take quite a few days and while drying is in progress an intense mushroomy smell will pervade wherever you are drying them.

In recent years, fruit dryers and

in strings in the kitchen. It is important to remember, however, that mushrooms such as morels could well have creepy-crawlies hiding inside so partially dry them somewhere before hanging them in your kitchen. This will prevent any wildlife dropping into your food. When the mushrooms are dry, carefully lay them on a sheet and pick the individual specimens over before placing them in airtight containers for storage. Don't waste any powder that

tion on the most suitable method for each species is given in the relevant individual entry.

Whatever method of storage you are going to use, it is important to select the very best of the mushrooms you have collected. Do be careful to make sure that they are completely free of insects because there is nothing worse when reconstituting dried mushrooms to find you have insects floating on the top of the water in which they are being reconstituted. Also make sure there are no twigs, leaves or other debris among them.

Drying preserves the flavor and color quite well, although unfortunately it often destroys the shape of the mushroom. There are several methods of drying. In warmer climates, slicing the mushrooms and

drying machines have become available. Some can take up to ten trays and are capable of drying a large quantity of wild mushrooms very effectively over several hours. The advantage of this is that it prevents the whole house smelling of mushrooms for days afterwards, and you can also be totally confident that your dried mushrooms are completely free of moisture. With this accelerated form of drying it is possible to dry even shaggy ink caps, so long as you use very young specimens. Ordinary drying methods are much too slow and they would collapse into an inky mess and probably ruin any other mushrooms you were drying with them.

Another effective way of drying mushrooms is to thread them with a needle and cotton and hang them up

may remain on the sheet, it can be stored separately and used to flavor soups and stews.

Dried mushrooms can be put directly into soups and stews, but for other dishes it is best to reconstitute them in lukewarm water for around twenty minutes. Do not use boiling water as this will impair the final flavor. The water in which they have been reconstituted can be used as stock or to make gravy, but, before you do so, pour it through a strainer to remove any extraneous matter or grit that might have been contained within the mushrooms.

An alternative to drying is freezing. Perhaps surprisingly, this is not a very good method of preserving mushrooms. For best results, make up the mushroom dishes and then freeze the finished dish or make up

**RIGHT** *Mush-rooms that have been dried and preserved for later use.*

**OPPOSITE FAR LEFT AND MIDDLE** *It is essential to brush and wipe clean mushrooms before they are dried or stored.*

**OPPOSITE NEAR RIGHT** *A mushroom drier.*

mushroom butter. To do this, slice your mushrooms, add them to melted butter and freeze the result. Preserved like this you have the mushrooms and the butter for use with sauces, to flavor various dishes and to add to your meat or fish dishes as a topping.

Salting is one of the oldest methods of preserving food. It works extremely well for mushrooms. The most important thing to remember is to have clean, fresh mushrooms. The quantities required are one part salt to three parts mushrooms. It is important to layer the mushrooms and salt alternately, and make sure the final layer of mushrooms is completely covered with salt. Use containers that the salt will not corrode. Although a sterilized jar is best, you could also use plastic containers.

When preserving mushrooms in this way you will eventually have a lot of seasoned juice and you will not need to use salt in any dish you make using salted mushrooms.

Mushrooms can be pickled in either oil or good vinegar. It is most important when using this method to clean the mushrooms well and then blanch them. If you are pickling them with vinegar, remember that the better the vinegar, the better the results will be, so it is not worth putting good mushrooms in inferior vinegar. The same applies if you are pickling mushrooms in oil. It is also a good idea to put peppercorns and half a dozen cloves of garlic into each jar, together with two or three bay leaves. Make sure the containers you use have a good seal, and when they are filled, seal tightly.

Once the seals have been broken, use the contents fairly quickly. And it is a good idea to keep the container in the fridge while you are doing so. Even when you have finished the mushrooms, the oil or vinegar in which they have been stored will make a wonderful dressing. If you preserve mushrooms by pickling, you must remember to sterilize everything you use. You can do this by immersing all your utensils in boiling water, or by using a sterilizing solution. Boiling water is probably best as there is always a danger that the sterilizing solution might affect the taste of the mushrooms. Remember, too, to keep a watchful eye on your pickled mushrooms for any sign of moldiness. If there is, discard the top few mushrooms and use the rest fairly quickly.

# Edible
# Mushrooms

# INTRODUCTION

This section illustrates and describes the best of the edible mushrooms that grow in our fields and woods. There are in fact over a thousand edible species and but only a small proportion of these are prized for their flavor and texture, and although personal taste will vary many consider the finest to include the cep *Boletus edulis*, bay bolete *Boletus badius*, morels *Morchella elata* and *esculenta*, chanterelle *Cantherellus cibarius* and chicken of the woods *Laetiporus sulphureus*. To enable identification each entry has a description of the mushroom in question, information on its habitat and season of growth, as well as hints on storage and cooking preparation for when you return home with a full basket.

As you learn about mushrooms you will become more respectful of the rules of identification. No mushroom looks exactly like another, and sometimes the differences are great within the same species. Many species have poisonous lookalikes, which are also mentioned here. Take particular care with such mushrooms. It is also essential that you never pick immature specimens for identification, because only with mature specimens can you be sure of an accurate identification.

Mushrooms are quite rich and even edible ones can cause stomach upsets. Some people seem more prone to these than others, so be careful if you are serving a mushroom dish to guests.

Although cultivated mushrooms can be eaten raw, all others should be cooked first. Mushrooms such as honey fungus *Armillaria mellea*, wood blewit *Lepista nuda*, field blewit *Lepista saeva*, and the morels *Morchella elata* and *esculenta* all contain a small amount of poison which is removed by cooking.

One of the best ways to learn about mushrooms is to go on a foray led by an expert. Not only will you have the chance to question the expert about the location, type and size of the various mushrooms that you find, but, at the end of the foray, you will have a chance to examine what everybody else has found and have them identified by the expert. In this way you will have an opportunity to see far more species than you would if you had just gone out collecting on your own. Forays are run by many organizations, including mycological societies, local nature trusts and local experts who organize them on an ad-hoc basis. Details of forays can usually be found through these groups and they may also be advertised in the local paper.

Enjoy your mushroom collecting, but don't take any risks with mushrooms you cannot identify.

**PREVIOUS PAGE** *Beefsteak fungus,* Fistulina hepatica. *Although these mushrooms are usually found at the base of tree trunks they can grow high up on the branches.*

**LEFT** *Field blewit,* Lepista saeva.

**OPPOSITE** *Amethyst deceiver,* Laccaria amethystea, *is a tasty mushroom that has a long season from late summer to early winter.*

*Agaricus arvensis*
# HORSE MUSHROOM

This is one of the larger varieties of mushroom. It is quite meaty in texture and has a very distinctive anise smell. Horse mushrooms are best picked when they are young because not only are they soon attacked by insects, but also the flesh becomes dark brown with age and will turn any cooked dish muddy brown in color.

*mature gills
turn dark brown*

*sometimes slightly
scaly cap surface*

*ring still attached
to cap margin*

26

These mushrooms tend to come up in the same fields year after year, so having once found a good growth of horse mushrooms keep watching in future years.

The horse mushroom often has yellowish markings on the cap. When you find one like this, check it particularly carefully to ensure that it is not, in fact, the yellow stainer, *Agaricus xanthodermus*, which will make you very ill if you eat it. This mushroom is dealt with in detail in the section on poisonous mushrooms so you can compare the two. Unlike the yellow stainer, the horse mushroom does not color when pressed or cut; the yellow coloring of the cap is its natural color.

### IDENTIFICATION

The cap can be from 4–9¾ in across. It is domed at first, but eventually expands to a fully convex shape. It is white but yellows with age. The stem is 3–4 in and has a large double ring. It may become hollow with age. The gills, which are white at first, turn a delicate pink and eventually dark brown in mature specimens. The flesh is thick and white but darkens with age and can become a little woolly lower down the stem. It has a distinct smell of anise. The spore print is dark brown.

### HABITAT AND SEASON

Horse mushrooms favor grassland and pasture, particularly, as the name suggests, that where cattle or horses have grazed. Grassy roadsides are often good places to look. The season is from midsummer to quite late autumn and they often grow in quite large rings.

### STORAGE

These mushrooms dry well, but it is important to check thoroughly that they are insect free. Slice and then dry either with open driers or with an electric drier.

### PREPARATION AND COOKING HINTS

These mushrooms make wonderful meals, provided, of course, that they are not infested with insects. Remember, too, if you are using older specimens when the flesh has turned dark brown, that they will change the color of your dish.

**ABOVE** *The yellow stainer.*

**ABOVE LEFT** *The horse mushroom prefers open meadows or woodland edges.*

**BELOW** *This specimen has a fully expanded cap when mature.*

## *Agaricus augustus*
# THE PRINCE

The prince is a good mushroom to find: not only does it look attractive, but it also has a lovely flavor and tastes delicious. These mushrooms grow in deciduous and coniferous woodland, and in dense groups rather than rings, in western North America.

### IDENTIFICATION
The cap is 4–9¾ in across. Button-shaped at first, it opens to a convex form and is often irregular in shape. It is light brown in color and has clearly marked rings of brown fibrous scales joining in the center. The stem is 4–7¾ in, off-white with small scales and a large floppy ring. The gills are off-white at first, turning dark brown with age. The flesh is thick, white and smells mushroomy. The spore print is brown.

### HABITAT AND SEASON
The prince grows mainly in coniferous and deciduous woods, often in clumps. The season is late summer to late autumn.

### STORAGE
As these mushrooms grow fairly large, make sure you have good specimens before slicing and drying them in the usual way. This is a good mushroom to store for winter use as it has an intensity of flavor which will enhance any mushroom dish.

### PREPARATION AND COOKING HINTS
A nice mushroom that needs very little preparation. The stem tends to be quite fibrous, so is best discarded. The cap does not need peeling, just wipe lightly with a damp cloth before slicing. The prince makes an extremely good addition to omelets, but is also nice on its own.

cap surface always with flattened scales

**ABOVE** *The prince is usually found at the edges of woods, clearings or pathsides, rarely very far from trees.*

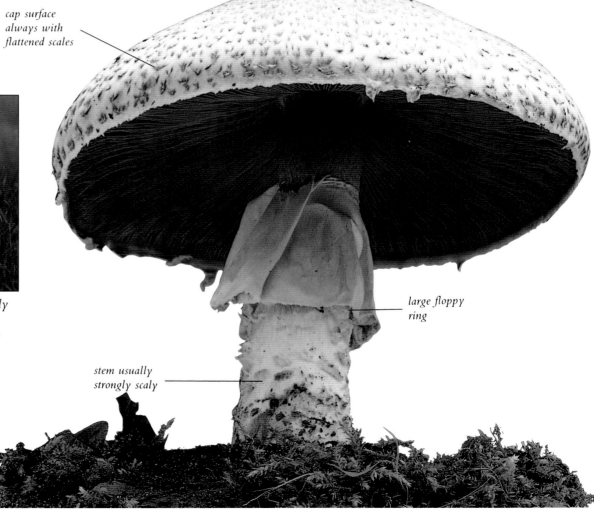

large floppy ring

stem usually strongly scaly

## Agaricus bisporus

*Agaricus bisporus* smells and tastes very similar to the field mushroom. It is believed to be the species from which most of the cultivated varieties come. It can grow in quite large quantities and is mostly found on wasteground and compost heaps. It is quite common.

### IDENTIFICATION

The cap is 2–4 in across, button-shaped before opening almost flat. It is whitish to mid-brown in color with flaky scales. The stem is 1¼–2 in and white, with a distinct ring below the cap. It has pink gills which become darker with age. The flesh is white, bruising slightly reddish and it has a distinct mushroomy smell. The spore print is brown.

**ABOVE AND BELOW** Agaricus bisporus *is the species that cultivated varieties come from. The button, cup and flat mushrooms, that are widely available, are the different stages of growth of this mushroom.*

### HABITAT AND SEASON

It grows on compost heaps, in garden waste and beside roads, occasionally on the edges of hedges and small plantations, but very rarely in grass. The season is quite early in the spring through to late autumn.

### STORAGE

This mushroom tends to be quite small and dries well, either whole or cut. It is full of flavor.

### PREPARATION AND COOKING HINTS

Because this mushroom often grows on compost heaps or in rough ground, it is best to wipe the cap very thoroughly, cutting off the bottom of the stem and slicing through.

*Agaricus campestris*

# FIELD MUSHROOM

The field mushroom is probably the best known of all wild mushrooms. Years ago fields were often carpeted with these small white mushrooms, but due to changes in farming technology and the greater use of herbicides, pesticides and, particularly, nitrates, many of the wonderful pastures where field mushrooms grew have disappeared. If you are lucky enough to have some old meadows and pasture near you, keep an eye open for a wonderful feast that can come at any time from quite early in the summer through to autumn. These mushrooms are best picked early in the morning, not only to beat other mushroom collectors, but also to ensure that they have not yet been attacked by insects.

## IDENTIFICATION

The cap is 1¼–4¾ in across. It retains its dome shape for some time before opening out fully. It is silky white, ageing to light brown. The stem is 1¼–4 in, white, tapering to the base,

gills are
pink when
young

ring is fragile
and often missing

**LEFT** *An example of a typical cultivated edible* Agaricus *species.*

**RIGHT** *Note that the gills are not attached to the stem, this is common to all Agaricus.*

**BELOW** Agaricus campestris *varies widely in nature and scaly forms are known as shown here.*

and has a thin ring which is often torn away. Even in unopened field mushrooms the gills are deep pink, an excellent identification feature. The white flesh bruises slightly pink. It has a pleasant smell. The spore print is brown.

### HABITAT AND SEASON
Field mushrooms grow in mature pasture and often favor alkaline soils. They can grow any time from early summer through to late autumn.

### STORAGE
An excellent mushroom for storing dried as it retains its flavor extremely well. The smaller specimens can be threaded on string and dried whole, but larger ones should be sliced.

### PREPARATION AND COOKING HINTS
These do not need peeling, a wipe with a damp cloth is sufficient, but do check them carefully to make sure there is no insect infestation. The best way to do this is to trim the stem carefully and slice through the center – any insects will then be easy to see. The older specimens are best used for sauces and stews, as these give a quite intense, dark brown color to the dish. Young specimens can be used as you like. They are delicious on their own or for breakfast with bacon and eggs.

## *Agaricus macrosporus*

This is quite a common autumn mushroom. It grows in rings and is extremely good to eat. Some care over identification is necessary, because it can look like the poisonous yellow stainer. However, the shape of the cap and, in particular, the smell are reliable aids to ensuring you have the right mushroom.

### IDENTIFICATION
The domed cap is 3–4 in across. It is off-white with light brown scales. The scaly stem is 2–4 in long, off-white and quite thick, with a slightly pointed base. The gills are pale pink at first, turning darker brown with age. The flesh is white and has a fairly distinct smell of almonds. The spore print is brown.

### HABITAT AND SEASON
Grows in rings in mature pastures that have not been treated with chemicals. The season is from late summer to autumn.

**RIGHT** *Often very large, the white cap may develop fine scales on the surface, as here.*

*thick ring with scaly under-side*

*gills free from the stem*

### STORAGE
This mushroom is very good to eat. It is best dried for storage, but specimens can be quite large so it is important to slice them first.

### PREPARATION AND COOKING HINTS
Clean the stem carefully and brush the cap: peeling is usually unnecessary. Check your specimens carefully, especially the larger ones, which may have become insect-infested.

## *Agaricus silvaticus*

This is a mushroom of mainly coniferous woodland, which grows in the same places year after year. It is also extremely good to eat.

### IDENTIFICATION

The cap is 2–4 in across, convex and covered with brown scales which give it an overall broken pattern. The stem is 2–3 in, whitish, but striated with brown markings; it has a brown ring. The gills are pale cream at first but turn quite red with age. The flesh is white and stains bright red when cut at the base or lengthwise. It has very little smell. The spore print is brown.

### HABITAT AND SEASON

The usual habitat is coniferous woods and the season is from early summer to late autumn.

### STORAGE

This mushroom has quite an intense flavor. It is best dried, but as it is often large, it should be sliced first.

### PREPARATION AND COOKING HINTS

Because this mushroom grows mainly in coniferous woods, the top will need to be brushed and any pine needles removed. Cut off and discard the lower portion of the stem and slice. It will give a wonderful flavor to your dishes. It is also good on its own, lightly sautéed with a little butter and basil, and served on toast.

*ring with small scale on underside*

*scaly cap surface scratches red*

*Agaricus silvicola*
# WOOD MUSHROOM

The wood mushroom has many similarities to the larger horse mushroom but, as the name suggests, it grows almost exclusively in woodland. Take care, however, not to confuse it with either the yellow stainer, *Agaricus xanthodermus*, or some of the deadly *Amanitas*. Check identifying features carefully. It does not grow out of a volval cup, so there will be no sign of one, and if you turn the mushroom over or cut it you will quite clearly see the identification features. If in any doubt, leave it alone.

### IDENTIFICATION
The cap is between 2–4 in across, domed at first before opening out to be almost flat. It is a creamy yellow which darkens with age. The stem is 2–3 in, quite thin and with a clearly marked ring. The gills are mid-pink before turning dark brown. The flesh is white and has a distinct anise smell. The spore print is dark brown.

### HABITAT AND SEASON
The wood mushroom is quite common in coniferous and deciduous woods. Its season is the autumn.

### STORAGE
These mushrooms do not store well, so use and enjoy them as soon as possible after you have picked them.

### PREPARATION AND COOKING HINTS
The young specimens are particularly tasty. Try coating the caps of young mushrooms in seasoned flour, dipping them in a batter made with beer or ale and then deep frying them: delicious.

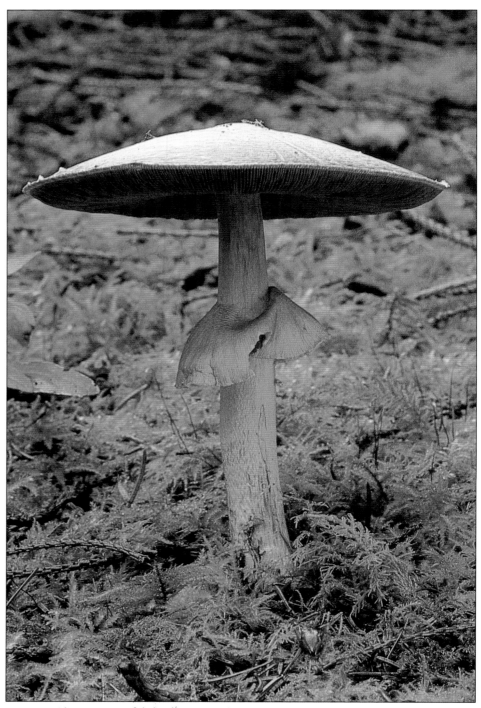

**ABOVE** *Always a graceful slender mushroom, the wood mushroom grows exclusively in woodlands.*

*Aleuria aurantia*
# ORANGE PEEL FUNGUS

This wonderfully bright fungus has a nice taste and texture. It is a useful addition to all wild mushroom dishes.

### IDENTIFICATION
The cap is small, just under ¼–2 in across; it is cup-shaped and becomes quite wavy at the edges. The inner surface is bright orange in color. The underside is much lighter and almost velvety to the touch.

### HABITAT AND SEASON
The orange peel fungus grows in fairly large clumps on almost bare earth in light grassland, along roads and in lawns. It is quite common and the season is from autumn through to early winter.

### STORAGE
Drying is the best method of storage.

### PREPARATION AND COOKING HINTS
Apart from cleaning it carefully, the orange peel fungus needs very little done to it. It is fairly tough, so can be lightly rinsed in water, then sliced thinly and added to your wild mushroom dishes, to which it will add both flavor and color.

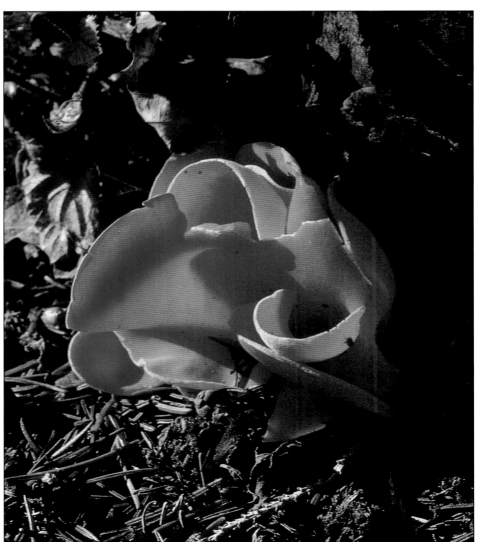

**ABOVE RIGHT** *Often growing in large clusters, the orange peel fungus prefers disturbed soils along paths and tracks.*

**RIGHT** *The inner surface (the hymenium) contains the spore-producing cells which are called asci.*

## *Armillaria mellea*
# HONEY MUSHROOM

The honey mushroom (*Armillaria mellea* and closely related species) is the dreaded enemy of the gardener. This mushroom grows from black cords known as rhizomorphs which can travel enormous distances. They kill the host tree and infect large areas of woodlands. It is, without doubt, the most dangerous of all the tree parasites, causing intensive rot and a very untimely death. If you find hon-ey mushrooms growing in your garden get expert advice fast. However, honey mushrooms are extremely good to eat and grow in very large quantities during the autumn.

### IDENTIFICATION
The cap can range from ¾–7¾ in across and is also variable in shape and color. It starts by being convex, then flattens and is centrally depress-ed. The color varies from almost honey to dark brown. The stem is 2–6 in and can vary quite consider-ably in width, sometimes being quite tuberous and at others very slender.

*tiny scales at cap center*

*yellow-white, cottony ring*

*stem bases fused together*

The ring is always clearly visible. The gills vary from off-white to dark brown. The flesh is white with a smell that is quite strong and sweet. The spore print is off-white. It is now thought that there are five or six different forms of honey mushrooms. They usually grow in large clumps, either on dead tree trunks, tree stumps or living trees.

## HABITAT AND SEASON
Honey mushrooms are fairly widespread in deciduous and coniferous woods, infecting living trees as well as dead trunks and stumps. The sea-

**ABOVE** *The scales of the cap vary considerably, ranging from almost smooth as seen here to quite coarse.*

**BELOW** *When old, the gills can be quite brownish but the spores are pale cream.*

son is from early summer to early winter and they can appear several times at the same place during a season.

## STORAGE
Drying tends to toughen this mushroom, so it is best to make up dishes first and then freeze them.

## PREPARATION AND COOKING HINTS
Only the caps are edible – the stalks are very tough. If you have any allergic reaction, boil the caps for two or three minutes in lightly salted water, which must then be discarded as the mushroom may contain a mild toxin. Then cook as you wish. After the initial cooking the caps are particularly good sautéed lightly with onion, garlic and basil, thickened with a little cream and served with pasta.

*Auricularia auricula*
# TREE EAR OR WOOD EAR

A common fungus with a very long growing season. It has some looka-likes, so take care with identification.

### IDENTIFICATION
The fruit body of the tree ear is ¾–2¾ in across with a jelly-like tex-ture and an ear-shaped appearance. In dry weather it becomes hard. It is tan-brown with small grayish hairs on the inner surface.

### HABITAT AND SEASON
Grows on a wide variety of trees, sometimes on elder trees: it gets its old nickname Judas' Ear from Judas Iscariot who was said to have been hanged on an elder tree. It has an extremely long growing season and therefore can be collected throughout the year.

### STORAGE
Best dried. In fact, if they are picked during dry weather when they are hard, they can be stored immediate-ly. Before using, reconstitute by put-ting in lukewarm water.

### PREPARATION AND COOKING HINTS
Wash thoroughly with several changes of water. As they have a gelatinous texture it is important to cook them well. A very nice way to serve them is to make a sauce with onions, garlic, basil and sliced tree ears, thickening it with a little cream, and using it to fill small patty shells or to spread on toast points.

*velvety
outer surface*

*inner surface appears
smooth and rubbery*

**LEFT** *If in doubt of your identification of this species, try stretching it between your fingers, it should be elastic and rubbery rather than brittle.*

**BELOW** *The color can vary greatly. These specimens are very young and fresh and so are quite pale: they may become quite purple-brown with age.*

## *Boletus badius*
# BAY BOLETE

**ABOVE** *Bay boletes found under conifers (left) are usually darker, smoother and*

*more maroon-bay in color than those found in deciduous wood (right).*

Bay boletus does not become infested with insects as much as some of the other boletes, but it is still best to pick only clean specimens. The flavor is excellent.

### IDENTIFICATION
The cap is 1½–7 in across, it is usually pale to mid-brown, although lighter specimens may be found. It has a polished appearance, and feels tacky when wet. The stem is 1¾–5 in and similar in color to the cap. The pores are light yellow, but stain blue if pressed or cut, which is one of the principal identification features of the bay boletes. The white flesh has a faint mushroomy smell, and also stains blue when cut, but the stain soon fades. The spore print is light brown.

### HABITAT AND SEASON
In all types of mixed woodland. The season is early summer to late autumn.

### STORAGE
A very versatile mushroom. Small specimens may be stored in jars of extra virgin oil, or in wine or cider vinegar. Larger specimens, however, are best sliced and dried after the

pores have been removed, because these will be quite wet and will not dry satisfactorily. These pores can be used in a mushroom sauce if you are making one at the time.

### PREPARATION AND COOKING HINTS
Bay boletus are best picked when they are dry. Wipe the caps of any wet specimens and let them dry before dealing with them. However, fresh or dried, the bay bolete is very versatile and can be used in many wild mushroom dishes.

*blue-grey stains when bruised*

*flesh may stain pale blue*

*no network on stem*

## *Boletus chrysenteron*
# RED-CRACKED BOLETE

Although the flavor of this boletus is not as good as that of the bay boletes or the cep, young specimens are good in mixed mushroom dishes.

### IDENTIFICATION
The cap is 1½–4 in across, light reddish-brown in color, but cracks in the surface of the cap often reveal a slightly reddish hue below. However, the red markings on the stem are the real giveaway of this bolete. The stem is 1½–3 in with a distinct reddish tinge for most of its length. The pores are yellow and much more open than those of the bay bolete; they stain a light greenish color. The flesh is cream to yellow and does not bruise on cutting. The spore print is light brown. The overall texture of this mushroom is much less dense than either the bay bolete or the cep.

### HABITAT AND SEASON
Found in association with all broad-leaved trees. The season is throughout the autumn.

### STORAGE
Dry this mushroom before adding it to your other dried mushrooms.

### PREPARATION AND COOKING HINTS
Only pick young specimens, wipe or brush the cap to remove any loose particles of earth and slice thinly before cooking. However, because it can be a little mushy, it is best used in soups, stews and mixed dishes with other mushrooms and not on its own.

**ABOVE** *As the cap ages, particularly in colder weather, the entire surface may take on a reddish flush.*

*red flush in cracks*

*yellow pores*

## Boletus edulis
# CEP OR PORCINI

Mushroom hunters regard this mushroom as a great prize; it has a wonderful nutty flavor and is extremely versatile. It can also grow very big and weigh as much as 2 lb 2 oz. It grows over a number of days and flies enter at the base of the stem and the insects work their way up to the cap and tubes so it is important to pick only those in prime condition. When collecting large specimens cut the cap in half to make sure there is no insect infestation before putting it in your basket.

### IDENTIFICATION

The cap ranges from 2½–11¾ in across. Its light brown color looks rather like freshly baked bread. The color darkens as the cap opens, and it is at this stage that you should examine specimens for insect infestation. In wet weather the cap can have a slightly sticky appearance, but in dry weather it has a nice velvety sheen. The stem varies from 1¼–9 in. It is very bulbous and has a fine network, with markings that are more pronounced towards the cap.

*yellow pores*

*white unchanging flesh*

The pores are white at first, turning light yellow with age. The flesh is quite white and does not change as the mushroom ages. The spore print is light brown.

### HABITAT AND SEASON

Coniferous, broad-leaved and mixed woodland; also beside grassy paths. It can also be found in association with heather, along with dwarf willows. The season is summer to late autumn and it is quite common.

**LEFT** *Ceps are a great culinary delicacy and they are considered at their best for eating when they are small and tight.*

**RIGHT** *A very variable species, some have swollen stems with much darker caps, particularly when found under conifers.*

*white network
on stem*

## STORAGE

Cut into thin slices this is probably the most important commercially dried mushroom in the world. Take your cue from this – drying is the best method of home storage. Small specimens can be kept in extra virgin olive oil, but it is really best to leave them so that they can grow on to more mature, and larger, specimens.

## PREPARATION AND COOKING HINTS

Clean the caps well and cut in half to check for insects before putting them in the basket. Brush the stem, cutting off the bottom or scraping it to remove any earth or fibers at the base. This is one of the most versatile mushrooms and it can be used in many cooked dishes.

## *Calocybe gambosa*
# St George's Mushroom

As its name suggests, St George's mushroom tends to appear around 23 April, St George's Day. It has a great variety of uses and is particularly welcome because it appears early in the year, at much the same time as the common morel. It frequently grows in rings which can be very large, although broken in places. The largest rings may be several hundred years old.

### IDENTIFICATION

The cap is 2–6 in across with a slightly inrolled margin. Well round-ed when young, large old specimens develop an irregular, wavy cap. It is white to cream in color. The stem is ¾–1½ in and white. The gills are narrow and crowded. The flesh is white and soft. It has a mealy smell which is pleasant and strong. The spore print is white.

### HABITAT AND SEASON

Tends to grow in rings in grassy locations and around wood edges with underlying chalk. The season is from the beginning of April and into May. For good growth St George's mushroom relies on warmth and moisture so if the spring is cold it will not appear until the weather becomes warmer. Keep checking areas where you have seen it before.

**RIGHT** *The caps vary from white to a creamy yellow color.*

**BOTTOM** *In these mature specimens note how the caps are irregular and wavy.*

### STORAGE

St George's mushroom dries extremely well. It can also be stored in virgin olive oil or in vinegar.

### PREPARATION AND COOKING HINTS

Brush the caps well because they can be quite gritty and dirty and there may be chalk particles on the underneath. When picking this mushroom always cut the stem to avoid damaging the mycelial rings. It goes particularly well with chicken and fish. If you can get this mushroom, which is very rare in North America, try it in a chicken casserole.

## *Cantharellus cibarius*
# CHANTERELLE

The excitement of finding this mushroom is, for many, the highlight of the mushroom season – not only does it look beautiful, it tastes wonderful. Most collectors are secretive about their chanterelle patches because these mushrooms grow year after year, often in abundant quantities. It is, however, important to be sure you have found the true chanterelle and not simply the false chanterelle, *Hygrophoropsis aurantiaca*.

### IDENTIFICATION
The cap is ¾–4¾ in across. Flat at first with a broken margin, it later becomes quite fluted with a central depression. The color can range from very pale to deep yellow, fading a little with age. Occasionally specimens are almost orange. The stem is 1¼–3 in, very solid and tapered towards the base. The yellow gills are blunt, narrow, irregular and run

cap depressed
when older

thick pale-yellow
flesh

blunt forking
gills or ridges

**LEFT** *The gills run down the stem and are the same color as the cap.*

down the stem. The yellowish flesh has a lovely faint fragrance of apricots – another important identification feature. The spore print is pale cream color.

### HABITAT AND SEASON

In all kinds of woodland which have open mossy clearings. The season is early summer to late autumn.

### STORAGE

All forms of storage can be recommended for the chanterelle. It is a particularly interesting one to store in spiced liquor because of its very fragrant flavor, but it is equally good stored in extra virgin olive oil or vinegar, or else dried.

### PREPARATION AND COOKING HINTS

It is important to clean chanterelles well when you pick them. Brush the caps, and wipe them with a damp cloth if necessary. Cut the stem to avoid any dirt getting into your basket. The chanterelle has a good shelf-life: specimens can be kept fresh for

some time either in a refrigerator or in a cool, airy place. They taste exquisite and are extremely versatile, whether on their own, in mixed mushroom dishes or with meat or fish dishes. They also give an elegant

color to sauces and the overall appearance of a dish. Try mixing all different types of *Cantharellus*: this will combine the different flavors and textures and make a brilliantly colorful dish of wild mushrooms.

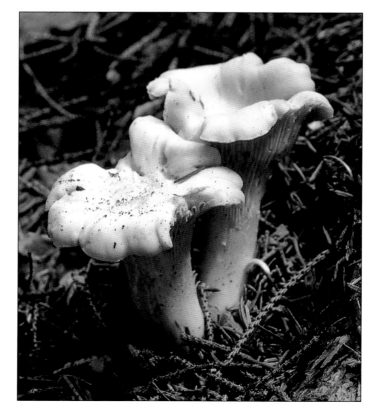

**LEFT** *Observe how the gills of this species are very shallow, blunt and frequently forked, more like deep wrinkles or veins than true gills.*

*Cantharellus infundibuliformis*

# WINTER CHANTERELLE

The winter chanterelle is so called because it usually appears much later than the ordinary chanterelle. It is quite an achievement to find these tiny little gems hidden under falling autumn leaves. But once you get your eye in, you will find groups of them growing where before you had hardly seen anything. They tend to grow in the same place each year, so note where you find them.

## IDENTIFICATION

The cap is ¾–2 in across, convex at first, soon becoming funnel-shaped with a fluted edge. It is dark brown on top, very much the same color as the leaf cover under which it grows. The stem is 2–3 in, yellow and hollow. The gills are narrow and quite irregular, yellowish at first they are

grayish-lilac forked gills or wrinkles

_hollow stem_

_brown cap surface_

grayish lilac in older specimens. The flesh is yellowish and smells faintly sweet. The spore print is yellow.

### HABITAT AND SEASON

Grows in large numbers in both deciduous and coniferous woods, preferring acid soil. The season is from late summer to late autumn.

### STORAGE

Winter chanterelles dry extremely well, but can also be stored in extra virgin olive oil or wine vinegar.

### PREPARATION AND COOKING HINTS

As these usually grow through leaf mold they are quite clean, so all they are likely to need is a dusting with your brush. And if you cut the stalks rather than pulling them up, you will avoid earth and other debris. They are very versatile in cooking, with an extremely nice, sweet flavor that goes especially well with fish.

**ABOVE** _A good tip for finding these mushrooms is to follow woodland streams and search on the mossy banks, as this is one of their favorite habitats._

**ABOVE** _When growing in fallen leaves, winter chanterelles are very difficult to spot._

49

# ANISE MUSHROOM

The aniseed toadstool is most useful as a condiment. Be careful when you identify it, because the verdigris agaric, *Stropharia aeruginosa*, looks rather similar, although it has a blunt knob at the center when open, and is always sticky and darkish-green in color. As the name suggests, the anise mushroom has a very pungent anise smell.

**IDENTIFICATION**

The cap is 1¼–2¾ in across; button-shaped at first, it soon flattens and sometimes becomes wavy. The color is a blue-green which darkens with

*cap surface is dry, not sticky*

*gills are pale greenish-white*

*no ring on stem*

RIGHT AND BELOW *This lookalike,* Stropharia aeruginosa, *has a sticky cap and a ring on the stem. It has no odor. The gills turn purple-brown when mature.*

**BOTTOM** *The color may fade rapidly from that shown to almost white. These specimens are best avoided in case of confusion with the suspect* Clitocybe fragrans, *which is white and also smells of anise.*

age. The stem is 1¼–2½ in and lightly striated. The gills, which are not very marked, are close and run down the stem. The flesh is pale and the smell is strongly of anise. The spore print is white.

### HABITAT AND SEASON

In leaf mold along the edges of coniferous and deciduous woods. In the latter they are likely to be in association with beech or oak. The season is from late summer to late autumn and they are relatively common.

### STORAGE

Best dried and stored separately because of the intensity of its flavor.

### PREPARATION AND COOKING HINTS

The anise mushroom is best used as a flavoring: finely chop fresh specimens or pulverize dried ones.

*Coprinus comatus*
# SHAGGY INK CAP

One of the most common mushrooms, they often come up in dense clusters on newly turned earth in meadows and gardens throughout the summer. Only the young specimens are edible and once picked they must be used quickly, otherwise they soon decay into a nasty inky mass. This is an easy mushroom to identify as it is very distinct, although care must be taken that the early stages of this and the magpie fungus, *Coprinus picaceus*, are not mistaken. However, the magpie fungus has some veil-like patches covering the cap which the shaggy ink-cap does not.

## IDENTIFICATION
The cap is 2–4¾ in across; egg-shaped at first, it opens into a bell. White with a cream-colored center; it has large shaggy scales. The stem is 4–14½ in and white. The gills are white to start with, slowly changing to black from the edge inwards before becoming a mass of ink which, incidentally, makes good drawing ink. The flesh is white with a slight sweet smell. The spore print is brown-black.

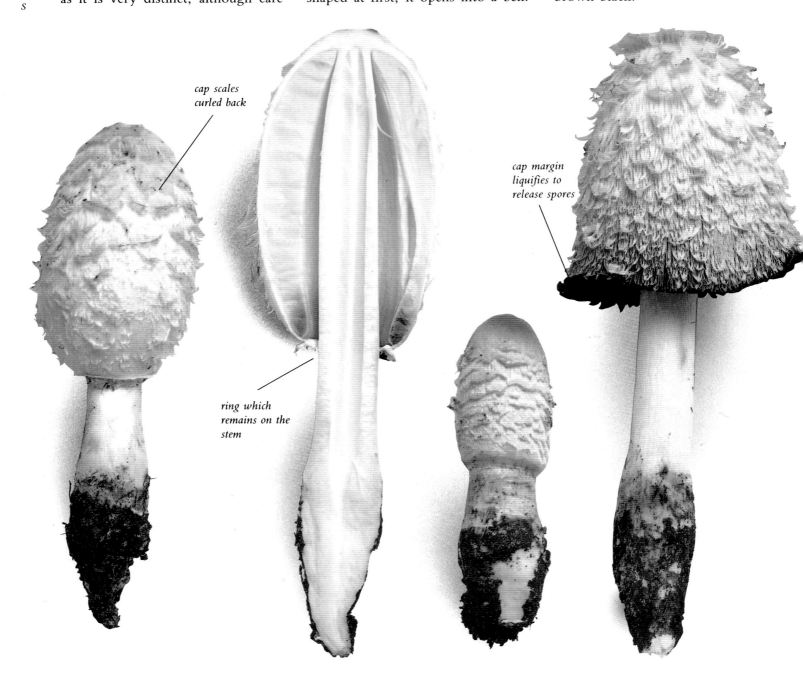

cap scales
curled back

cap margin
liquifies to
release spores

ring which
remains on the
stem

## HABITAT AND SEASON

Widespread on grassy banks beside roads, on compost heaps, lawns and recently disturbed soil near building sites. The season is midsummer to late autumn. They are very common.

## STORAGE

Best used fresh or dried in an electric drier. Do not attempt to air-dry them as they will turn into an inky mass.

## PREPARATION AND COOKING HINTS

Although shaggy ink caps can be used dried; they are really best fresh, either on their own, or with the parasol mushroom, *Macrolepiota procera*, to make a wonderful soup. Use the two mushrooms, some onions and a little potato to thicken, sweated together and then puréed. Simple and quite delicious.

**BELOW** *The very distinct narrow ring is not easily seen here, but as the cap expands it will be left behind on the stem.*

**ABOVE** *This is the best stage to collect shaggy ink caps for cooking.*

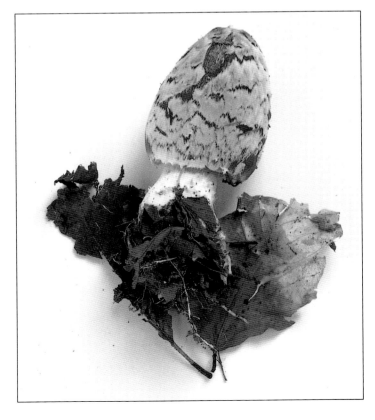

**LEFT** *Magpie fungus,* Coprinus picaceus *can be confused with the shaggy ink cap in its early stages.*

## *Craterellus cornucopioides*
# HORN OF PLENTY OR BLACK TRUMPETS

Another wonderful mushroom of the *Cantharellus* family. Like the chanterelle and winter chanterelle, the horn of plenty appears in large groups in the same place year after year. These, however, are quite often covered by dead leaves and are difficult to spot because of their color. Although the initial appearance is not inviting, the taste is excellent.

### IDENTIFICATION
The cap is ¾–3½ in across; it is shaped like a tube or a trumpet and has an open flared mouth and is hollow. It becomes irregular with age and is thin and tough. In color it ranges from mid-brown to black, though it fades with age. The gills are barely perceptible. The flesh is grey to black. The spore print is white.

### HABITAT AND SEASON
Grows in large clusters among the dead leaves of deciduous woods. The season is from late summer to quite late autumn.

### STORAGE
All forms of storage are appropriate for the horn of plenty, but it is probably best dried.

smooth to
slightly wrinkled
surface

trumpet-like
depression

## PREPARATION AND COOKING HINTS

Remember that these mushrooms are hollow. You will always need to brush them and, with larger specimens, it is best to slice them in half and remove any debris that has gone down the funnel-cap. The horn of plenty is very versatile in cooking, but goes particularly well with fish, its dark color making a striking contrast with white fish.

*completely hollow*

**BELOW** *Like the winter chanterelle, this species is found in damp mossy banks alongside streams and in deep leaf mold.*

## *Fistulina hepatica*
# BEEFSTEAK FUNGUS

An important bracket fungus from a collector's point of view, not only is it interesting in color and texture, it has a good flavor. Because the beefsteak fungus often grows fairly high up trees, you may well need to add a ladder to your collecting equipment.

### IDENTIFICATION
The bracket can vary from 3–11¾ in across and is quite thick. It is usually in a single piece, although several may grow one above the other. Cut through, the beefsteak fungus really does look rather like a piece of meat. The color of the bracket is an orange-red darkening with age, the pores are much lighter. The flesh is thick, succulent and mottled dark red; it has quite a pleasant smell. The spore print is brown.

### HABITAT AND SEASON
Grows on oak trees, usually, but not always, on the lower part of the trunk. Season is late summer to autumn, although it may appear earlier. Although this fungus causes rot inside a tree it does not kill it, but it makes the wood of infected trees much darker. Oak darkened in this way is in demand in the furniture

*cut flesh "bleeds" red juice*

*pores pull apart very easily*

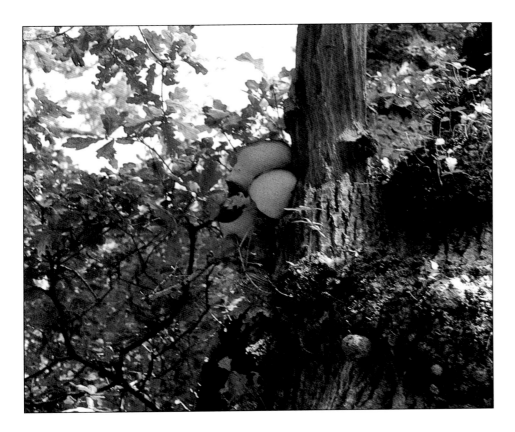

LEFT *Beefsteak fungi often grow very high up in trees. Another good clue to identifying this species is that the individual tubes separate from each other very easily, unlike all other bracket fungi.*

BELOW *The upper surface can be very moist and spongy when fresh.*

industry. Near Holt, in north Norfolk, England, there is a 980-year-old oak tree with beefsteak fungus growing up to a height of 40 ft from the base, a little bit difficult from a picker's point of view, but nevertheless a wonderful sight.

### STORAGE

Like other bracket fungi this will toughen if dried, so it is best to make dishes and then freeze them.

### PREPARATION AND
### COOKING HINTS

Cut off any parts of the tree still attached to the fungus. Separate the various layers and wipe them with a damp cloth. The beefsteak fungus has a slightly metallic taste, so it is best to slice it into strips and soak these in milk for about two hours to remove the slight acidity and acrid flavor. Then it can be broiled like a piece of steak with a little onion, basil and garlic. Try it, too, on a charcoal grill or barbecue. It is also excellent added to soups and stews for extra flavor and color.

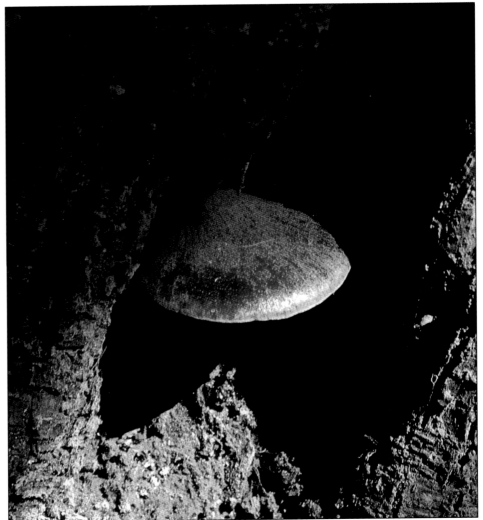

## *Flammulina velutipes*
# VELVET SHANK

As the name implies, the velvet shank has a dark velvety stem. It normally grows during the winter months and can survive the frosts, indeed it may need a frost before starting to grow. It can be frozen solid, but still survive.

### IDENTIFICATION
The cap is 1¼–4 in across and fairly flat. It is light orange in color, paler at the edges and darker towards the center. It is also quite smooth and shiny with a sticky surface. The stem is ½–1¼ in, very tough and is, as the name suggests, velvety and dark in color, particularly at the base. The flesh, which is yellow on the cap changing to dark brown on the stem, has little smell. The gills are pale yellow. The spore print is white.

### HABITAT AND SEASON
The velvet shank often grows in very large clusters on dead or decaying wood, particularly in association with elm and oak. The season is long because they grow all through the winter months in more temperate zones and so are useful when only a limited number of mushrooms is available.

### STORAGE
The best method of storage is to dry and pulverize them.

### PREPARATION AND COOKING HINTS
As they have a fairly tough texture they really are best dried. If using them fresh, cut off most of the stem, and slice the caps finely. Use to give a good flavor to soups and stews, but remember to cook them well.

dense clusters of stems

black, velvety stem base

no ring on stem

**LEFT** *Difficult to confuse with anything else because of the unusual season of growth but note the absence of a ring on the stem. Poisonous lookalikes will have a ring or a veil.*

## *Grifola frondosa (syn. Polyporus frondosus)*
# HEN OF THE WOODS

This is an unusual fungus which, like the cauliflower fungus, grows at the base of tree trunks and can be extremely large. Its many caps are joined together and a large specimen can provide a feast for many people. Good to eat and quite rare, so note where you find it as it will certainly grow there again.

### IDENTIFICATION
The fruit body is 4–6¾ in across, and consists of a central section with many branch stems ending in individual caps. Each cap is 1¼–2¾ in across and has quite a wrinkled edge. The whole fruit body is grayish in color turning brown with age. The stems are pale gray. The hen of the woods has tubes rather than gills. These are ¹⁄₁₀ in long and run down the stem. The flesh, which is white, has a slightly musty smell.

### HABITAT AND SEASON
Hen of the woods grows at the base of the trunks of oaks or other deciduous trees. Occasionally it grows on tree stumps. The season is autumn to early winter.

### STORAGE
The best method of storage is drying. Otherwise freeze dishes in which you have used this mushroom.

### PREPARATION AND COOKING HINTS
It is important to clean the hen of the woods thoroughly as it has many nooks and crevices which harbor dirt. Due to its very tough texture it can be rinsed in cold water prior to cooking. It tastes good and goes well in a wide variety of wild mushroom dishes, but, because of its tough texture, make sure it is well cooked. Dried and then powdered, it can be added to soups and stews.

## *Hydnum repandum*
# HEDGEHOG FUNGUS

This little gem is often quite difficult to find on the woodland floor. Perseverance pays as it has great culinary value and is much sought after by collectors.

### IDENTIFICATION

The cream-colored caps are usually single and ¾–6 in across, flattening with a slight central depression and rolled rim. The stem is 1¾–3 in and quite bulbous. It is quite downy, and is white, bruising slightly yellow when cut. In place of pores or veins, this mushroom has little spines, hence the name hedgehog fungus. The flesh is white with a very pleasant smell. The spore print is cream-colored.

### HABITAT AND SEASON

Grows in large numbers and under deciduous or coniferous trees, usually in quite damp sites such as along drainage ditches or where there are mossy patches. The season is late summer to late autumn.

### STORAGE

These are best sliced and dried for winter use, although they can be kept in oil or vinegar.

### PREPARATION AND COOKING HINTS

After cleaning, the smaller specimens can be cooked whole or else sliced. With larger specimens it is probably best to remove the spines, as although quite edible they look like small hairs and could spoil the appearance of the finished dish. This is a very versatile mushroom, going very well with both meat and fish dishes, but it is worth trying some on their own for their excellent flavor.

spines on underside of cap

very thick tough stems

thick, peppery tasting flesh

**LEFT** *The cap color can vary from pinkish-buff to this rare white form.*

# Hygrophorus nemoreus

BELOW *The different stages of development are clearly shown: with a bell shape at the beginning, the cap spreads with a very clear, round central area.*

E
D
I
B
L
E

M
U
S
H
R
O
O
M
S

Most *Hygrophorus* (250 species) have bright colors and often have a viscous or sticky cap. This species is an exception with a rather dull color and a dry cap.

### IDENTIFICATION
The diameter of the cap is between 3–4¾ in. It is at first bell-shaped, then flattened, maintaining a darker umbo. The fibrillose-striate top is usually matt and dry. The color is cream at first. The gills become pink or pale orange when older. The stem is whitish or pale brown like the cap but lighter. It is pointed at the end and often curved. Its surface is, on the whole, fibrous but shows around the top a floury-granular zone, that is to say granulose dots. The flesh is white and tender with a slight smell of flour.

### HABITAT AND SEASON
Grows in deciduous woods in autumn.

### STORAGE
Drying is a good way to store this

species because of its soft and delicate flesh. To be sure the mushrooms do not contain any pests, it is advized to cut them longitudinally before cutting or slicing them. After that thread the pieces onto a string or lay them on a tray.

### PREPARATION
Clean your mushrooms "on site" and transport them carefully as they are very fragile.

*The gills are well-spaced.*

*The base of the stem is pointed.*

*Laccaria amethystea*

# AMETHYST DECEIVER

The amethyst deceiver grows in large groups. It is colorful, edible and tasty, and so makes excellent additions to your cooking.

### IDENTIFICATION
The cap is ½–2 in across. It is convex but flattens with age and develops a slight depression in the center. Deep purplish-lilac in color, it dries to an almost buff color. The stem is 1½–4 in, hollow and has slightly white fibers below the cap. The gills are a similar color to the cap. The flesh is thin and tinged lilac. The smell is not distinctive. The spore print is white.

### HABITAT AND SEASON
Grows in coniferous and deciduous woods, often with beech. The season is late summer to early winter. It is very common.

### STORAGE
Dries very well. It can also be stored in spiced liquor to give a most unusual sauce to serve over ice cream and desserts.

### PREPARATION AND COOKING HINTS
As these grow quite densely and have wide open gills, they can be dirty, so it is important to clean them well before using. If you store them in spiced liquor, blanch them first. It is important that if stored in liquor these are kept in a refrigerator to prevent fermentation. They are also excellent fresh.

*cap becomes much paler when dry*

**LEFT** *When picked, amethyst deceivers are bright in color but this will fade.*

## *Laccaria laccata*
# DECEIVER

Like the amethyst deceiver, the deceiver grows in large groups.

### IDENTIFICATION
The deceiver has a cap that can be slightly larger than the amethyst deceiver, but is also convex and flattening. It can open to look like a chanterelle. The color is tawny to pale red and it dries to a paler color. The stem is 2–4 in, a similar color to the cap, but often is twisted. The gills are well spread. The flesh is a pale reddish-brown and the smell is not distinctive. The spore print is white.

### HABITAT AND SEASON
Grows in coniferous and deciduous woods. The season is late summer to early winter. They are very common.

### STORAGE
The best method of storage is drying.

### PREPARATION AND COOKING HINTS
Like the amethyst deceiver, it is important to clean it well before putting it in your basket. Follow the instructions on the opposite page for spicing in liquor.

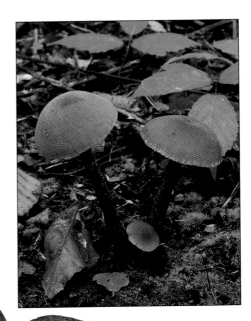

**RIGHT ABOVE AND BELOW** *The deceiver is incredibly variable and it may take you many seasons to recognize the many variations.*

## *Lactarius deliciosus*
# SAFFRON MILK-CAP

A lovely, colorful mushroom to find. It grows very close to the ground and often on quite sandy soil, which can make cleaning difficult. It also has a hollow stem which can lead to problems with infestation. To avoid this problem just pick young fresh specimens, but at the same time make sure that they are mature enough for a positive identification, otherwise they can be confused with the woolly milk-cap, *Lactarius torminosus*, or *Lactarius pubescens*, both of which are poisonous.

**ABOVE** *As you can see, the cap becomes pale, almost silvery-white or dull greenish with age. Pick the fresher orange caps.*

### IDENTIFICATION
The cap is 1¼–4¾ in across, convex with a depressed center. It has concentric rings and, as the name suggests, is saffron in color. On cutting

cap with
concentric rings

stains green
when bruised

bleeds orange
milk when cut

you will notice that it bleeds a saffron color. It also has a clean, inrolled edge. This is an important means of identification, because neither the woolly milk-cap nor *Lactarius pubescens* have clean edges to the cap. The hollow stem is 1¼–2½ in pale, blotched with orange, and when bruised or broken, turns greenish. The closely spaced gills are saffron in color. The flesh is pale. The saffron milk-cap is brighter in color than either of its lookalikes, which is a useful aid to identification.

### HABITAT AND SEASON
Always grows under pine or spruce trees, and can also be found beside paths on sandy terrain. The season is early summer to quite late autumn.

### STORAGE
This stores extremely well, whether dried or in oil or vinegar.

### PREPARATION AND COOKING HINTS
The sand and pine needles of this mushroom's habitat make cleaning important. Indeed, it may be necessary to wash your specimens immediately before cooking, but then dry them well before slicing and cooking them. The lovely crunchy texture and good flavor make this a much sought-after mushroom.

**BELOW** *In young specimens the margin is involuted.*

**RIGHT** *The cap margin is shaggy in these young specimens.*

*Laetiporus sulphureus*

# SULPHUR POLYPORE OR CHICKEN OF THE WOODS

One of the more spectacular of all bracket fungi, this can grow in very large quantities and come quite early in the mushroom season. Its versatility makes it important from a culinary point of view, but only pick young specimens.

### IDENTIFICATION

The bracket can range from 6–19¾ in across. Often the shape of a fan, it has a semi-circular growing habit and softly rounded edges. The color is spectacular; lemon to orange-yellow, although it tends to darken with age. The brackets have an almost velvet-like appearance. It has yellow tubes. The flesh in young specimens is ten-der and exudes a yellow juice. The smell is quite pungent and a little acrid.

### HABITAT

Grows on deciduous trees, particularly oak but may also be found on yew, cherry and willow. The season is usually from late spring to early autumn, but if the winter has been mild it will often appear much earlier depending on the zone, so keep a look out for it.

### STORAGE

Drying toughens this mushroom, so it is best used fresh and the finished dish frozen.

### PREPARATION AND COOKING HINTS

Avoid the toughest specimens and only use young ones. Cleaning can be difficult but it is best to separate the individual layers, brushing light-ly; bearing in mind that the dense texture makes it possible to wash it to remove any infestation or dirt. If you notice a slight bitter taste blanch it for two to three minutes in boiling, salted water prior to cooking. The texture and flavor is of chicken, as the name suggests, and it is much prized by chefs. It is wonderful for vegetarian meals, making an excellent chicken of the woods risotto or chicken of the woods curry.

**BELOW** *The giant polypore, Meripilus giganteus, can reach 3 ft across. Its flesh stains black when bruised but it is edible when very young.*

**BELOW LEFT OPPOSITE AND BELOW** *When young, the strange lumpy growths of Laetiporus sulphureus look quite unlike the elegant brackets it will form with age.*

**BOTTOM** *This bracket lasts quite a while in the field and when old is soft, spongy and paler in color. Pick brightly colored fruit bodies.*

*Langermannia gigantea*
# GIANT PUFFBALL

The giant puffball can be truly spectacular. It is also versatile in the kitchen, but only pick specimens that are fresh and young and sound hollow when you tap the top of the mushroom. It is pointless picking this mushroom once the flesh has become discolored. Check its age by cutting the specimen right through; the knife should not tear the flesh but pass crisply through it.

### IDENTIFICATION
The fruit body can range from 2–31½ in across, although specimens of 48 in across have been recorded. When young it has a clean white appearance, although the outer wall may break away to expose the spore mass and become yellow. Avoid at this stage.

**LEFT** *Hedges and ditch banks are the favorite habitats of the giant puffball.*

*solid white flesh when young*

## HABITAT AND SEASON

The giant puffball grows in gardens, pastures, woodlands and a wide variety of other situations, such as along stream banks. The season is any time from early summer to late autumn unless the weather is very dry, when it will not grow. There will usually be several in the same area and they grow in the same place year after year after year.

## STORAGE

There is no satisfactory way of storing giant puffballs, so it is best to make up the dishes and freeze them.

## PREPARATION AND COOKING HINTS

Very little needs to be done to this mushroom. Wipe the specimens carefully with a damp cloth and, if you are not going to use them immediately, wrap in a paper bag and keep in the refrigerator for up to three days. The giant puffball goes extremely well in all wild mushroom dishes, soups and stews. It also makes a good breakfast sliced and fried with bacon or else dipped in beaten egg and breadcrumbs and lightly fried in bacon fat or corn oil.

**LEFT AND ABOVE** *This shows another large edible species,* Lycoperdon excipuliforme, *which frequently grows in large clusters. It is common in woodlands.*

## *Leccinum scabrum*
# BROWN BIRCH BOLETE

*flesh may redden in some forms*

*slightly sticky smooth cap*

Although the brown birch bolete is not as well favored as the orange birch bolete, it is still quite useful in the kitchen. However, only pick young firm specimens as older ones tend to absorb a good deal of moisture and so have a very soft texture.

### IDENTIFICATION
The cap is 2–4¾ in across and mid-brown in color. It is dry, but can be slightly sticky in wet weather. The stem is 2¾–7¾ in, white with brown to blackish flecked scales. The pores are brown. The flesh is white and the smell quite pleasant. The spore print is brown.

### HABITAT AND SEASON
Grows under birch trees. The season is summer to late autumn.

### STORAGE
Drying is the best method of storage. Cut it into sections and either air-dry or use an electric dryer.

### PREPARATION AND COOKING HINTS
As this mushroom has quite a soft texture, it is best to use it in conjunction with other mushrooms in a mixed mushroom dish or in mushroom soups.

**RIGHT** *The brown birch bolete has recently been subdivided into a number of closely related species, all of which are edible.*

## *Leccinum versipelle*
# ORANGE BIRCH BOLETE

A bolete that is particularly good to eat. It can grow to a fairly large size and, as the name implies, is usually in close association with birch trees.

### IDENTIFICATION

The cap is 2½–9¾ in across. It is a lovely orange color and has a slightly fluffy appearance at first before becoming smooth or scaly, depending on the weather conditions. It is usually dry. The stem can be up to 7¾ in. It is white to grayish in color and covered with brown to blackish scales. The stems of young specimens bruise a bright electric blue in patches. The pores are off-white to gray. The flesh is pale, becoming blackish with age. The smell is quite pleasant. When cut in cross-section this mushroom stains quite black on the inside, but you should not be put off by this as it is good to eat. The spore print is light brown.

### HABITAT AND SEASON

Grows in association with birch and scrub. The season is midsummer to quite late autumn.

### STORAGE

Because this mushroom can be quite large, it is best to slice it before drying, which is the best way of storing it.

### PREPARATION AND COOKING HINTS

It should only be necessary to wipe the cap with a damp cloth and brush any loose dust particles from the stem. A versatile mushroom, it is much sought after by chefs.

*flesh turns reddish-lilac then black when cut*

*stem scales darken with handling*

*leaves of birch, the preferred host tree*

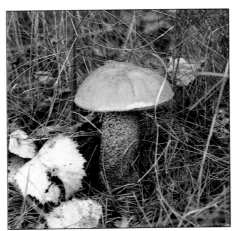

**ABOVE** *The caps may expand to a much greater size in proportion to the stem than is shown here and the color can fade to dull yellow buff.*

**ABOVE** *The cap may become quite felt-like and scaly with age, particularly at the center.*

## *Lepista nuda* (syn. *Clitocybe nuda*)
# WOOD BLEWIT

The wood blewit is useful because it appears late in the season. But beware – some people are allergic to it. Make sure you try only a little first and take care if you serve it to guests. It is also most important to remember it must be well cooked and never eaten raw.

**IDENTIFICATION**

The cap is 2½–4¾ in across. Convex at first, it eventually flattens and is sometimes quite irregular. The cap starts by being quite blue but then turns an almost shiny tan. It dries a little paler. The stem is 2–3½ in and often has purple markings. The gills are crowded and very lilac, although they lose their color with age they never turn brown. It is best to pick younger specimens that still retain the wonderful color for they have the best flavor. The flesh is bluish and the smell is quite perfumed. The spore print is pale pink.

*gills remain violet, never turn brown*

*smooth cap surface*

*tough, fibrous stem*

## HABITAT AND SEASON

Grows in all mixed woodland, hedges and gardens and sometimes on open ground. The season is from autumn to early winter. It is quite common and often grows in large quantities.

## STORAGE

Because the wood blewit must be cooked before it is eaten, it is best not to dry it. It does, however, keep extremely well if it is blanched and then put in wine vinegar, extra virgin olive oil or spiced liquor. But, if kept in the liquor, it must be stored in the refrigerator to stop fermentation. The color and fragrance of this mushroom mean it can be used in both sweet and savory dishes.

## PREPARATION AND COOKING HINTS

Quite an easy mushroom to clean, gently wipe the top and cut the stem. It is good in all mushroom dishes, but as it has a very strong flavor it goes particularly well with strongly flavored vegetables such as onions and leeks. Try a blewit bake by mixing onions, leeks and wood blewits in a béchamel sauce. Do not forget, however, that some people are allergic to it.

**TOP** *Note that the caps are smooth and not sticky. The gills remain violet, never turning rusty brown as do those of some lookalike species, such as* Cortinarius.

**RIGHT** *Although these specimens are under pines, the blewit is equally common in deciduous woods and gardens.*

## *Lepista saeva*
# FIELD BLEWIT OR BLUE LEG

The field blewit is most commonly found exactly where the name suggests. But, because they are low-growing, they are difficult to spot in long grass. Its other name, blue leg, comes from the brightly colored stem. It is best picked young, to avoid infestation with insects. Remember, like the wood blewit, this mushroom must be cooked before it is eaten and some people are allergic to it, so take care.

### IDENTIFICATION

The cap is 2½–4¾ in across. Quite convex at first, then flattening, it can be slightly depressed when fully

*these are in perfect condition for picking*

opened out. The cap is a rather insignificant buff color, but it has a nice shine. The stem, which is 1¼–2½ in is the most significant thing about the field blewit. It is often rather bulbous and has lilac markings. The gills are crowded and whitish. The flesh is quite thick and chunky and white to flesh-colored. It has a perfumed smell very similar to that of the wood blewit. The spore print is pale pink.

### HABITAT AND SEASON

Often grows in large numbers in rings in pastures. The season is autumn through to the first frosts of winter, although it can stand some light frosts.

## STORAGE

As this is another mushroom that must be cooked before it is eaten, it is best blanched and stored in wine vinegar or extra virgin olive oil. Store in spiced liquor if you want to serve it as a dessert.

## PREPARATION AND
## COOKING HINTS

Very similar to the wood blewit, the field blewit gives a really good flavor to stews if it is chopped up first.

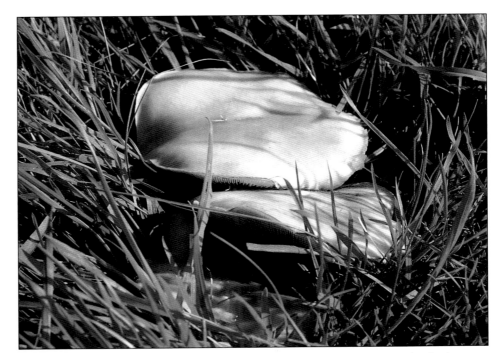

**ABOVE** *Here, you can see clearly the complete lack of violet color in the cap, compared to the wood blewit.*

*no violet in gills*

*bluish-lilac stem may fade when old*

## *Macrolepiota procera*
# PARASOL MUSHROOM

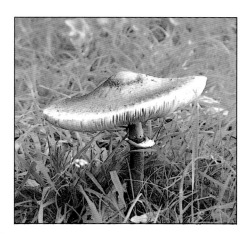

The parasol mushroom can grow quite large and has a long growing season. They reappear in the same place year after year, and may well have several fruitings during the season. The name is appropriate, as this mushroom does indeed look like a lady's parasol.

### IDENTIFICATION
The cap, which is 4–9¾ in or more, starts by being spherical, but soon flattens out, though retaining a prominent center. It is pale buff in color and covered with symmetrical patterns of dark shaggy scales. The stem is 6–11¾ in, white and has a large ring. The gills are white, becoming darker in age but never turning green. The flesh is thin and white and has a fairly sweet, although not particularly distinctive, smell. The spore print is white. This mushroom is usually insect-free and is best collected when dry as it soon absorbs moisture, becoming soggy and almost unusable.

### HABITAT AND SEASON
In open woods and pastures, and along roadside hedges. The season of the parasol mushroom is from early summer to late autumn.

### STORAGE
This mushroom dries well. Discard the stems, which are tough, cut the cap into segments and dry.

### PREPARATION AND COOKING HINTS
This mushroom is usually clean and insect-free, so very little attention needs to be paid to cleaning. However, dust off any particles on the top, remove the stalk right into the cap and cut into segments. An excellent, if unusual, way of using it is to make up a batter with beer or ale instead of milk, dipping the pieces into the batter and then deep-frying them. Alternatively, you can dust the segments of cap in seasoned flour and shallow- or deep-fry. Cooked like this it makes a crisp start to a meal or a good addition to a main course.

## *Macrolepiota rhacodes*
# SHAGGY PARASOL

The shaggy parasol is smaller than the parasol mushroom. Although it is edible it can cause stomach upsets, so serve to knowledgeable guests.

### IDENTIFICATION

The cap is 2–4¾ in across; ovate at first, it expands to become almost flat. It gets its name from the cap's shaggy appearance. The markings are not as clear as those of the parasol, but it has quite a fibrous appearance. The stem is 4–6 in, off-white with a pinky-brown tinge. The gills are white at first, becoming tinged with red as it ages. The white-tinged flesh bruises reddish-brown or pink. When cut it turns red. The smell is aromatic. The spore print is white.

*very coarse recurved scales*

### HABITAT AND SEASON

Grows in woods and shrubberies of all kinds, often with conifers as well as under hedges and along grassy roadsides. The season is early summer to late autumn.

### STORAGE

A mushroom that dries extremely well. Discard the stalk, cut the cap into sections and dry. Reconstituted, it is excellent in soups and stews or mixed wild mushroom dishes.

### PREPARATION AND COOKING HINTS

Very similar to the parasol. The shaggy parasol has a clean cap which needs very little attention other than a light brushing. If using fresh specimens, discard the stalk and cut the cap into segments, then deep fry or add to mushroom dishes. The smaller caps are good for stuffing.

**ABOVE** *The form shown here is the typical woodland type with dull-brown colors. In gardens a larger white form with very bulbous stem base occurs.*

*stem ages and stains brown*

*ring will be left around stem*

**LEFT** *The stems may be deep in leaf cover so look out for the bulbous base, which is a characteristic feature.*

*Marasmius oreades*

# FAIRY RING MUSHROOM

One of the first mushrooms to appear in spring, the fairy ring mushroom tastes just as good as it looks. But beware, there is a poisonous look-alike, the *Clitocybe dealbata*, that grows in a very similar way in very similar sites. It is most important to learn to identify these two. There is very little similarity once they are full grown, but it is important not to make any mistakes.

## IDENTIFICATION

The cap is ¾–2 in across, convex at first, then flattening with quite a marked center. Tan in color, it dries to a fairly light buff. The stem is ¾–4 in and tough, so it is best when picking to remove the stem entirely. The gills are white to tan and quite distant. The flesh is thick. The spore print is white.

## HABITAT AND SEASON

It forms rings in the shorter grass of old pastures or lawns. The season is from late spring to late autumn. It is very common. It is essential to be able to distinguish between this mushroom and *Clitocybe dealbata*. The latter also grows in rings, often very close, within a meter, to those of the fairy ring mushroom. The color and gills are quite different and *Clitocybe*

*dealbata* does not appear so early in the year, but it is most important that you can identify them.

*widely spaced
thick gills,
pale brown in color*

*gills do not
run down the stem*

*caps darker
when young*

*tough
fibrous stems*

78

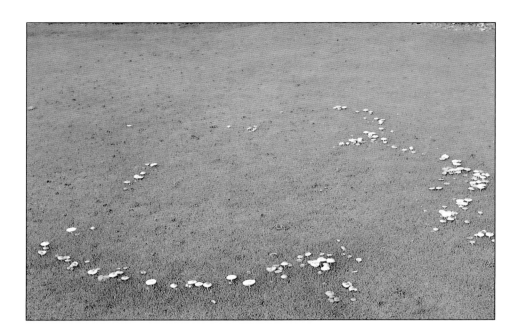

**LEFT** *This classic fairy ring is a few yards across, but they may reach over a hundred yards!*

## STORAGE

These mushrooms are wonderful eaten fresh, but also dry very well. They can also be stored in spiced red Vermouth, extra virgin olive oil or wine or cider vinegar after blanching.

## PREPARATION AND
## COOKING HINTS

As long as you pick these mushrooms clean and cut off the stems when picking them from grass, the only problem you are likely to have is removing a few blades of grass. Occasionally a light dusting with a brush may be necessary, but washing definitely spoils the flavor. From a culinary point of view this is a versatile mushroom, going extremely well with meat and fish dishes as well as mixed mushroom dishes.

**BELOW** *Note how the grass is shorter where the mushrooms are growing because the nutrients have been absorbed by the fungi.*

## *Morchella elata*
# BLACK MOREL

A member of the highly edible morel family. This, like *Morchella esculenta*, grows in the early spring, so keep an eye open for it as soon as spring arrives.

### IDENTIFICATION
*Morchella elata* is very similar to *M. esculenta* but much darker, often almost black with the ridges and pits aligned in vertical rows. The cap is often tall and pointed. The mushroom stands 2–6 in high.

### HABITAT AND SEASON
Grows in gardens, waste ground, along roadsides and disused railway lines. Season is throughout the spring.

### STORAGE
Like *M. esculenta*, the black morel is best dried.

### PREPARATION AND COOKING HINTS
Clean thoroughly before cooking, slicing the fruit body in half to make sure it is free of insects. Cook and serve as you would *M. esculenta* and, like that morel, it must be properly cooked before it is eaten.

*completely hollow cap*

**BELOW LEFT AND RIGHT** *Another similar morel is the common morel,* Morchella vulgaris. *Look closely at these two examples, their caps may be dark but they have completely irregular pits and ridges unlike the black morels.*

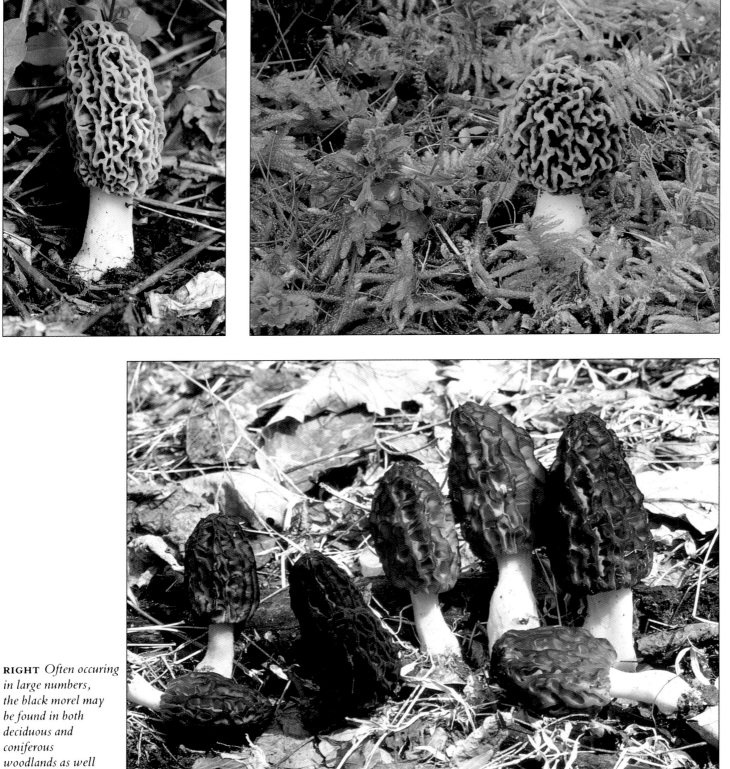

**RIGHT** *Often occuring in large numbers, the black morel may be found in both deciduous and coniferous woodlands as well as along paths and in gardens.*

## Morchella esculenta

The morels are among the most exciting springtime fungi. Careful examination of their habitat is necessary because they blend into their background so well. They usually grow singly; two or three can sometimes be found within a reasonably small area, but very rarely more. Excellent mushrooms from the culinary point of view, they must be cooked before eating – never, ever, eat them raw.

### IDENTIFICATION
The fruit body is 2–7¾ in high. Although very convoluted, with a honeycomb effect, the overall shape is pointed. It is palish brown in color and darkens to orange-yellow with age. Inside it is hollow. The flesh is white to cream.

### HABITAT AND SEASON
Found among shrubs or in open woodland, on waste ground, along path edges and often along disused railway lines. The season is throughout the spring. Wind is very important in spreading the spore of this fungus so, if you find a good specimen, follow the direction of the prevailing wind and you will often find some more.

### STORAGE
Best dried for storage. Because of all the nooks and crannies, this morel is often infested with woodlice and other insects so will need cleaning thoroughly before drying and storing.

### PREPARATION AND COOKING HINTS
The easiest way to clean this mushroom properly is to slice each one in half to make sure there is nothing hiding inside, rinse it in clear water and dry. One of the nicest ways to use fresh morels is to stuff the large fruit body. They also go well with meat dishes and provide a very rich sauce. Dried, the intensity of their flavor will enhance most wild mushroom dishes.

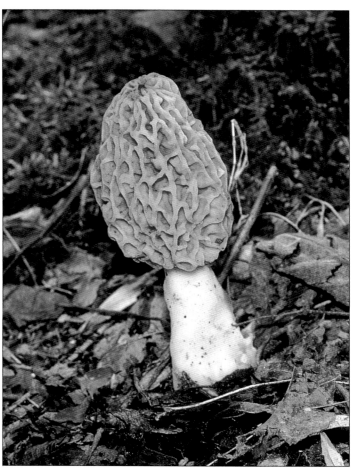

**ABOVE** *When young, the fruit body is often dull buff or brown in color with blunt ridges.*

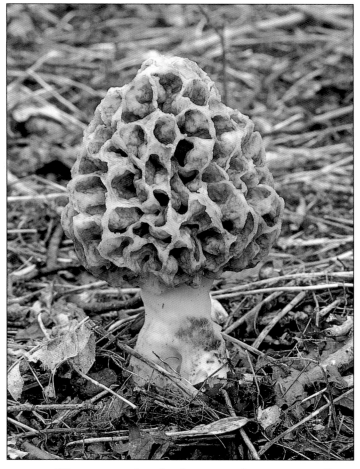

**ABOVE** *When mature, the color changes to ochre or orange-yellow and the ridges become sharper.*

old caps are
quite yellow

completely
hollow
cap and
stem

cap joins
stem without
overhang

stem base often
very swollen

pits and ridges
are very irregular,
never in vertical
lines as in the
black morel

young caps
very dark

## Pleurotus cornucopiae

This member of the oyster mushroom family is fairly widely spread. It can be found on the same trees and at the same time as the oyster mushroom, so always have a good look for it before you leave the tree.

### IDENTIFICATION
The cap is 2–4¾ in across and convex. It often makes quite a funnel-like shape, which frequently becomes fluted and split at the edges. Whitish in color, almost a magnolia shade, it turns a fairly dark brown with age. The stem is 2–3 in. Several fans may grow from the same stem, rather like flowers. The gills are quite deep and run down the stem; they are white to light tan in color. The flesh is white and has a rather mealy smell. The spore print is lilac.

### HABITAT AND SEASON
It grows in dense clusters on cut stumps of most deciduous trees, in particular elm, oak and beech. The season is spring to late autumn.

**BELOW** *The stems here are shorter than usual for they often reach 2–3 in in length. The way that the stems are fused together is quite characteristic.*

### STORAGE
This mushroom air-dries well.

### PREPARATION AND COOKING HINTS
If picked carefully, only a light wipe of the cap should be necessary. Discard most of the stalk as it will be quite tough, particularly where it was attached to the tree. The pleasant flavor makes it a good addition to all mushroom dishes.

*gills run down the stem*

*often deep funnel-like cap*

## *Pleurotus ostreatus*
# OYSTER MUSHROOM

**BELOW** *This is the gray-brown late-autumn/winter form of* Pleurotus ostreatus. *In summer, the cream-colored form,* P. pulmonarius, *is more common.*

Now grown commercially on a fairly large scale and so quite familiar, it is still exciting to find a wild oyster mushroom. They grow on dead or decaying trees, often in large masses. They will grow in the same place in successive years, so remember where you picked them.

### IDENTIFICATION
The cap is 2½–4¾ in across. It is shaped rather like a fan and larger specimens may have fluted edges. The color can vary: usually a slate gray, they can sometimes have a slightly brown or bluish tinge. They have almost no stem. The gills run down the stem; pure white at first, they turn cream with age. The flesh is white with a pleasant smell. The spore print is lilac. Oyster mushrooms grow in groups, one on top of the other, and if carefully removed from the tree are usually very clean.

### HABITAT AND SEASON
These occur in large clusters on standing trees or on the stumps of fallen trees. Most commonly found on beech trees, they will grow on other trees, especially elm. The season is all year round.

### STORAGE
All methods of storage can be used for oyster mushrooms. If you separate the caps you can air-dry them very successfully.

### PREPARATION AND COOKING HINTS
If picked carefully they are likely to be clean and a wipe with a damp cloth is probably all they need. The oyster mushroom's pleasant flavor means that it goes well with almost all meats and fish, making it extremely useful in the kitchen.

*stems may be absent*

*crowded gills run down the stem*

*Russula cyanoxantha*
# CHARCOAL BURNER

The charcoal burner is an excellent mushroom to eat. However, it is a member of a very large genus and identification within the group can be very difficult. Correct identification is essential because some are poisonous, in particular the beechwood sickener, *Russula mairei*, and the sickener, *Russula emetica*. As always, if in doubt leave it out.

## IDENTIFICATION
The cap is 2–7 in across and slightly greasy. Convex at first, it opens out with a shallow depression in the center. Occasionally a single color but more often than not quite a mixed shade, ranging from purple to light green, frequently with a rather faded appearance. The stem is 2–4 in and white. The gills do not run down the stem and are whitish or pale cream in older specimens. A clear identification feature of the charcoal burner is that the gills do not break away if they are touched, they are quite clearly joined to the cap margin. This is in marked contrast to some *Russula* species. The flesh is white and the smell is pleasant. The spore print is white.

## HABITAT AND SEASON
Usually to be found under broad-leaved trees, but can also grow in association with pine trees. The season for the charcoal burner is summer to late autumn and it can be very common.

## STORAGE
Drying is a very good method of storing the charcoal burner.

## PREPARATION AND COOKING HINTS
It is rare to find a perfect specimen, as woodland wildlife attack it from almost the moment it appears. As a result it will need careful cleaning. However, it is good to eat whether fresh or dried and will add an interesting taste and texture to your mushroom dishes, as it retains quite a crunchy texture when cooked. But do remember to be careful with your identification of the charcoal burner and make sure it is not one of the poisonous *Russula* species.

*cap is often of mixed colors or even green*

*stem is white, sometimes flushed lavender*

*crowded white gills*

**RIGHT AND BELOW** *The dull violet-purple cap shown here is typical, but beware, the cap can also be completely green. The best means of identification is to brush your fingers over the gills and they should be flexible and not crumbly as most other* Russulas *are.*

**BELOW** *A large and colorful group of mushrooms, all* Russula *species. The mushrooms in this family are some of the most difficult to identify accurately.*

*Sparassis crispa*

# CAULIFLOWER FUNGUS

The cauliflower fungus is quite unlike any other fungus you will find in the woods. When you find one you will understand why it got its name. It is quite unusual, but grows in the same place year after year, so make a note of where you find it. One large specimen can last for several days if stored carefully in a cool place with its base in water.

### IDENTIFICATION

The cauliflower fungus has no cap in the ordinary sense of the word, instead the fruit body is built up of many layers that resemble a cauliflower or a brain. A short stem attaches it to the tree on which it grows. The fruit body ranges from $7\frac{3}{4}$–$19\frac{3}{4}$ in in diameter. It ages from a pale yellow-white to brown. It has a sweet smell and a lovely nutty flavor.

### HABITAT AND SEASON

It grows on the roots of pine trees, very close to the trunks. Be careful not to cut too deeply when picking this fungus so as not to destroy the main mycelial growth from the roots; then you will be able to come back for more in subsequent seasons. *Sparassis crispa* is a western species; the eastern species is called either *S. spathulata* or *S. herbstii* and lacks a stem. It grows on old oak stumps as well as pine.

The cauliflower fungus grows from late summer to late autumn but is susceptible to frosts and so will be killed by the first frosts of winter.

### STORAGE

This dries extremely well. Air-drying is probably best: hang your specimens up on strings in a light, airy place for several days. Very large specimens can be cut into sections so they will dry more quickly. As the fungi dry the insects and other life in them will fall out, so do not attempt to dry them in your kitchen; an airy

*color varies from buff to creamy white*

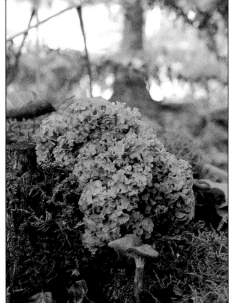

**LEFT** *Note the flattened crispy lobes. If they are pointed and branched you have probably mistakenly picked one of the* Ramaria *species which are often toxic.*

shed or outside storeroom would be best. Any hint of dampness will, of course, spoil the drying. It is very important to dry this mushroom thoroughly – be patient, it will be worth it.

**RIGHT** *The fruit bodies are almost always at the base of a tree or stump, as seen here.*

## PREPARATION AND COOKING HINTS

Pick only creamy white specimens, as this is when the fungus will be at its very best. Cleaning needs care as there are so many nooks and crannies in the cauliflower fungus and, as it grows so close to the ground pine needles can be a problem. If possible, avoid cleaning in water. It is better to brush away any dust particles, cut into thin slices and clean each slice before cooking. If you do use water, remember to dry the fungus well on paper towels before cooking. One of the nicest ways to deal with this fungus is to cut it in thin slices, dip them in a batter made with beer rather than milk and deep-fry to make a wonderfully crisp nutty hors d'oeuvres or accompaniment to a favorite dish. But it is equally good if sliced fresh and added to stews and casseroles.

*edges of lobes turn brown with age*

89

*Suillus luteus*
# SLIPPERY JACK OR PINE BOLETE

The slippery jack is quite common and a good find, although its open texture makes it prone to insect infestation. Much prized by chefs, it is very versatile in the kitchen.

### IDENTIFICATION
The cap is 2–6 in across; a nice mid-brown color with a marked sheen. It tends to be very sticky when wet, so is best picked in dry conditions. The stem is 2–4 in, pale yellow with a large, clearly visible ring. The pores are pale yellow. The flesh is white. It has no particularly distinctive smell. The spore print of the slippery jack is light brown. Only pick mature fresh specimens.

### HABITAT AND SEASON
Found in association with conifers, particularly Scots pine. The season is late summer to late autumn.

### STORAGE
Because of its soft texture, this mushroom is best thinly sliced and dried for use in winter dishes.

slimy surface when moist

pores unchanged by bruising

thick purple ring

## PREPARATION AND
## COOKING HINTS

As the cap is slightly sticky in texture it is best peeled before use. Check carefully for insect infestation. This mushroom exudes quite a lot of juice when cooking, so it is a good idea to sauté it out first on its own. Strain well and keep the resulting liquid to be used later for a sauce. Then add the mushrooms to other dishes. Slippery jack can be used in many ways. One nice one is to mix the strained mushrooms with rashers of broiled or fried bacon, add the strained juice, thicken with a little flour and serve it on toast.

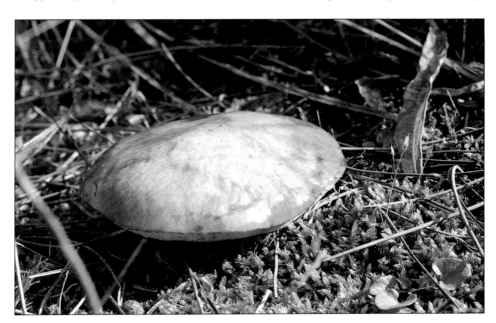

**BELOW** *This and other* Suillus *species are only found growing under conifers.*

**BOTTOM** *Observe how the cap colors change from young to old. The purple-brown turns pale to orange-brown with age.*

## Suillus variegatus

Another useful bolete to add to your collection, although it is not as good to eat as the cep or the bay bolete. Only pick young specimens. They are quite light in texture and therefore can become insect-infested, so check specimens before collecting.

### IDENTIFICATION
The cap is 2–4¾ in across and a rusty color. It is sticky when picked wet. The stem is 2–3½ in. The pores are quite clearly a snuff-brown color. The flesh is very white. The spore print is light brown.

### HABITAT AND SEASON
Found almost exclusively with conifers. The season is from late summer to late autumn.

### STORAGE
Best dried.

**BELOW** *The rough, almost dry surface of the cap is seen well here.*

*dry, slightly felted, scaly surface*

### PREPARATION AND COOKING HINTS
A wipe of the cap is usually all that is necessary, but beware when slicing specimens to look out for insect infestation. A good addition to mixed mushroom dishes.

*white flesh sometimes stains faintly blue*

*dark pores with smaller pores within the larger are very characteristic*

92

*Tricholoma ponderosa*
# WHITE MATSUTAKE

**BELOW** *This large species has a single layered ring at the stem apex, some lookalike larger species will have double rings at the top.*

This is one of the larger mushrooms and is much favored by the Japanese. It is excellent whether eaten fresh or dried.

### IDENTIFICATION
The cap is 1½–9¾ in across, convex becoming flat, with a broken margin. It is slightly inrolled at first, but opens fully with age. It has a smooth surface which feels quite tacky when dry. It is pale white and can be streaked with light brown. The stem can be up to 6 in; it is solid and is sheathed with a veil that runs from the cap to the base. It breaks in patches and can become pinkish-brown, and quite fibrous around the root. The gills are white, attached and crowded. The white flesh, which can stain light brown, has a slightly spicy smell. The spore print is white.

### HABITAT AND SEASON
It is scattered in coastal areas in sandy soil and is usually found in conjunction with conifers. Not known to grow in Europe, it is common in western North America. The season is late summer to mid-autumn.

### STORAGE
Drying is the best method of storage. Whole mushrooms can be dried quite easily, using an electric dryer, by hanging them up or by placing them on drying racks. Dried ones can often be found in Japanese and Chinese supermarkets.

### PREPARATION AND COOKING HINTS
Likely to be clean when you find it, it will need little more than washing. It adds an interesting flavor to wild mushroom dishes, but is quite strident, so be careful what you use it with and how much you put in a dish. As it has a large cap, it is also ideal to be used for stuffed mushroom dishes.

*Tuber aestivum*

# SUMMER TRUFFLE

Although summer truffles grow far more extensively than most people realize, finding them is difficult for they grow beneath the surface of the soil. Animals love them, particularly squirrels and deer, so watching them might give you a clue as to where to start looking.

### IDENTIFICATION

The fruit body is ¾–4 in across. It is irregular, though roughly globe-shaped, and covered in a host of tiny black warts. It is blackish-brown in color. When cut through, it reveals a wonderfully marbled, reddish-brown interior. The smell is very distinctive and sweet and the taste is nutty.

### HABITAT AND SEASON

The summer truffle favors calcareous soils and can be found in the ground near beech trees, and also, though less often, in association with sweet chestnuts and evergreen oaks. The season is late summer to autumn.

### STORAGE

One of the best ways of storing truffles is preserving them in olive oil. First of all clean the truffle and shave off the skin which can be used in future recipes. Blanch the truffles very quickly before placing in oil in a completely air-tight container.

### PREPARATION AND COOKING HINTS

As truffles have a very strong flavor they are best used in small amounts and even a tiny quantity can transform a dish. They are delicious served with egg and pasta dishes.

*spores are dispersed by burrowing animals and insects*

*Tuber magnatum*

# THE PIEDMONT OR WHITE TRUFFLE

This must be the prize for all mushroom hunters. The most sought-after of the truffles, it is found in very limited areas, mostly in northern Italy, where the finest certainly grow. Unfortunately, highly trained dogs or pigs are necessary to locate it.

### IDENTIFICATION

The fruit body is generally 2–4¾ in across, although much larger, tennis-ball-sized specimens do occasionally occur. It is irregular in shape and yellowish-brown in color. Indeed, in color and size it is not unlike a new potato. The flesh is marbled and has a slightly reddish-brown tinge. The smell is highly distinctive and sweet.

### HABITAT AND SEASON

Just below the soil surface in mossy mixed woodlands. Its season is from late autumn through the winter to early spring. Due to its intense smell, it is found usually by dogs or pigs.

### STORAGE

These truffles are best stored in closed containers and used fairly quickly after collecting. They have an intense flavor which can permeate foods, so use them to flavor eggs before cooking. Alternatively, put in a closed container with freshly made pasta and leave in the fridge overnight. This gives the pasta a most wonderful truffle scent. The best method of storage would definitely

be in extra virgin olive oil. It will not only preserve the truffle but will flavor the oil and give it a wonderfully rich truffle taste. These are the most valued of the wild fungi and command extremely high prices. Excellent quality ones can be obtained from specialty importers, and the truffle oil, the fresh truffles or the truffles in extra virgin oil are well worth buying.

### PREPARATION AND COOKING HINTS

Very little needs doing to the truffle beyond a careful brushing. If they are to be used fresh, very finely sliced slivers, quickly cooked, are best for the intensity of the flavor.

solid marbled flesh has strong odor

smooth but lumpy surface is characteristic

# Poisonous Mushrooms

# INTRODUCTION

Every year, in spite of repeated warnings, people die of mushroom poisoning. Such deaths emphasize the importance of identifying your mushrooms correctly. People often make the literally fatal mistake of assuming that if animals can eat a mushroom so can humans. Unfortunately this is untrue, for example, slugs eat death caps and other members of the genus *Amanita*. So do not be taken in when you see signs of either bird or animal activity; it is probably safe for them but may not be for you. Be particularly careful if dealing with the *Amanitas*, remember that their spores are poisonous and that if eaten they will cause extensive damage to the liver and central nervous system. If you think you are dealing with an *Amanita*, dig out the whole specimen with a stick to examine the volval cup. It is a good idea to protect your hand with a glove.

Never, ever, put a poisonous mushroom or an unidentified one with others in your basket. If you require a specimen for identification, put it in a separate container, and always wash your hands after touching any unidentified mushrooms. If you pick a deadly *Amanita* for display, throw out the mushroom and container immediately after use. A good way to transport and display such mushrooms is to put them in a plastic container on crumpled paper and to cover the whole box with plastic wrap. People can then see the mushroom without having to touch it. There are many old wives' tales about how to identify edible and poisonous mushrooms. They are all false. Particularly dangerous is the saying that if you can peel it you can eat it. You can peel a death cap, which got its name for a very good reason! Other sayings refer to staining silver spoons black. Ignore them all, and take great care over identification so that you can be sure of living to enjoy your mushroom trophies.

Between the good edible mushrooms and the deadly poisonous ones, there is an enormous range of other mushrooms regarded as inedible or not worthwhile. These are not all included in this book. Should you require information about them, consult one of the guides listed at the end of this book.

Although most people can eat the edible mushrooms and fungi identified in this book, it is important to remember that eating large quantities of any very rich food can often cause upset stomachs, and some people do have an adverse reaction to fungi. Among those that could cause problems are the wood blewit, *Lepista nuda*, and the field blewit, *Lepista saeva*. Should you ever become ill after eating mushrooms, it is important to see your doctor immediately. Mushroom poisoning can occur almost instantaneously or up to fourteen hours after eating the mushrooms, and at any time in between. It is imperative that you seek medical advice and, if possible, take a sample of the mushroom you have eaten. Correct identification of the poison could be life-saving, and there are many cases of *Amanita* poisoning being dealt with early enough to save the victim's life.

Another mushroom to beware of is the yellow stainer, *Agaricus xanthodermus*. A member of the genus *Agaricus*, it grows in similar situations to the ordinary field or horse mushroom and can be quite common in good mushroom years. Safety is the key for all collectors, so if you are not sure about a mushroom, leave it out of your basket.

**PREVIOUS PAGE** *A typical group of fly agarics,* Amanita muscaria, *showing how the red pigment fades at the edges with age or after rain.*

**LEFT** Clitocybe rivulosa, *similar to the fairy mushroom but highly toxic.*

**OPPOSITE** *The death cap,* Amanita phalloides. *The slight radial streaking on the cap can be seen well here.*

*Agaricus xanthodermus*

# YELLOW STAINER OR YELLOW-STAINING MUSHROOM

The yellow stainer accounts for approximately 50 per cent of the cases of mushroom poisoning among those who pick either field or horse mushrooms. It has an unpleasant smell and taste and must be avoided at all costs. Identification can be difficult and therefore take careful note of the identification features and illustrations. The symptoms of poisoning are sweating and flushing with unpleasant stomach cramps. Not everyone is affected by the yellow stainer, but it is not worth taking any risks – leave it well alone.

## IDENTIFICATION

The cap is 2–6 in across. Convex and angular at first, it flattens out later with a dip in the center. Very white

*intense yellow stains on surface when scratched*

*cap becomes grayish and slightly scaly with age*

*mature gills turn brown*

*thick ring joins cap to stem*

when young, it darkens with age as it expands to a fairly large cap with grayish-brown scales. It bruises a very bright yellow as soon as it is touched or cut, making this a valuable identification feature. Although this mushroom has many similarities with other members of the agaric family, the bright yellow staining is the giveaway. The stem is 2–6 in and white, staining bright yellow at the base. The gills are flesh-colored, darkening with age. The flesh is white. Smell is an important means of identifying this mushroom as it smells something like carbolic. The spore print is purple-brown. Should you have picked a yellow stainer by mistake and put it in your pan it will quite often turn the rest of the contents a slimy sickly yellow. It will also give off an acrid smell in the kitchen that is very unpleasant.

## HABITAT AND SEASON

The yellow stainer grows in woods, pastures and gardens. It has quite a long growing season, from summer to late autumn. It is common in certain areas.

*Amanita citrina* and *Amanita citrina* var. *alba*

# FALSE DEATH CAP

There are two forms of the false death cap, *Amanita citrina* and *Amanita citrina* var. *alba*. Although neither are deadly poisonous, they are so easily confused with the death cap that it is best to leave them alone.

### IDENTIFICATION

There are two distinct forms of this fungi: one with a pale greenish-yellow tinge to the cap (*A. citrina*) and the other with a pure white cap. (*A. alba*). In both forms the cap is 1½–4 in across. It is usually covered with patches of the veil, which is one of the features that distinguishes it from the death cap which rarely has any veil remnants. The stem is 2½–3 in. It has a large basal bulb or cup where the remnants of the veil can be seen and it has a clear ring around the stem. The gills are off-white at first, darkening with age. The flesh is white. The spore print is white.

### HABITAT AND SEASON

Grows in deciduous or coniferous woods, especially beech woods, but can be found in a large variety of locations. The season is from summer to late autumn and it is quite common.

**RIGHT** *The false death cap grows in both coniferous and deciduous woodlands. A pure white form is common under beech. A potato-like smell is typical.*

*veil fragments mostly washed*

*bulb with gutter-like margin*

**BELOW** *In this example, the prominent flat white patches of veil have washed off the cap leaving it quite smooth.*

*Amanita muscaria*
# FLY AGARIC

Without doubt this is everybody's idea of a toadstool or poisonous mushroom. The little flecks on the red cap which sometimes grows to 7¾ in across make it quite distinctive. Many fables of myth and magic are associated with this mushroom. One, which sounds like a myth but is not, is its use by the Sami people of Lapland to round up their reindeer herds. They take advantage of the reindeers' liking for the fly agaric and scatter dried ones for the reindeer to eat, which makes them more manageable. The toxins contained in *Amanita muscaria* attack the central nervous system producing intoxication, hallucination and a euphoria that is similar to drunkenness. The poison stays in the system for several months but the symptoms generally disappear in twelve hours, although it may take several days to fully recover.

The only mushroom you are likely to mistake for *A. muscaria* is *A. caesarea*. However, *A. caesarea* has a large volval cup whereas *A. muscaria* does not. In addition, when cut lengthways, *A. muscaria* is white whereas *A. caesarea* is yellow. Another pointer is that the cap of *A. caesarea* does not show flecks of the remnants of the volval cup. When the volval cup finally breaks, it leaves *A. caesarea* clean. *A. caesarea* grows in limited locations throughout Europe except the United Kingdom.

### IDENTIFICATION

The cap of the fly agaric is 3–7¾ in across, cup-shaped at first, it then flattens out. Although usually bright scarlet and covered with flecks of veil remnant, the color may fade in wet weather, and a few come up a fairly

*white gills do not join the stem*

*remains of veil*

**BOTTOM** *After heavy rain, the flecks wash off the cap of the fly agaric and the red color fades to orange.*

pale orange. The white stem is 3–7 in. If you take a specimen right out of the ground you will see the rounded, swollen stem base. (The gills are white.) The smell is indistinct. These often occur in fairly large groups at all stages of development. The spore print is white.

### HABITAT AND SEASON

The fly agaric is most often found with birch trees, although it can occur with a wide range of trees and in many locations. The season is late summer to late autumn and it is very common.

**BELOW** *One of the main distinctions between* Amanita muscaria *and* A. caesarea *is that* A. caesarea *has a large volval bag, similar to those shown in this picture of the* A. umbonata *but* A. muscaria *does not.*

*Amanita pantherina*
# Panther Cap

Less common than the fly agaric, the panther cap, *Amanita pantherina*, too, is severely toxic. The greatest danger with the panther cap is that it can be confused with the blusher, *Amanita rubescens*. Many people eat the blusher after first cooking it to remove the toxins and then using it normally. However, it requires a very expert eye to distinguish between young specimens of the blusher and the panther cap, so it is best to avoid both species for fear of making a mistake.

### IDENTIFICATION

The cap is 2–4 in across, almost bronze in color, and covered with small pure white remnants of veil. The margin also has remnants of the veil. The stem is 3½–5 in, white with a ring. It has a very bulbous base and narrow ring, very low down which

*narrow, hoop-like ring low down on stem*

*pure white fragments of universal veil*

*one or more rings of tissue around bulb-like base*

forms a distinct free rim around the base. There are usually also one or two belted rings immediately above the bulb. The spore print is white.

### HABITAT AND SEASON

The panther cap grows with both coniferous and deciduous trees mostly in western North America. The season is summer to late autumn, winter in California.

**ABOVE** *Beech woods on limestone soils are the favorite habitat of the panther cap although it will grow under coniferous trees as well.*

**RIGHT** *This picture illustrates the narrow hoop-like ring around the middle of the stem.*

*Amanita phalloides*
# DEATH CAP

Each year the death cap accounts for most of the fatal poisonings caused by eating mushrooms. It looks fairly innocuous, smells pleasant and can be peeled. However, it is deadly and only one cap is needed to cause serious, possibly fatal, poisoning. The range of colors can be quite dramatic, making identification even more difficult. It can vary from a sickly green to dark brown to pale white, so great care must be taken over identification. If you go on a foray, make sure the leader finds one to point out to you. If it is dug out of the ground you will see the volval cup at the base very clearly. Take a good look and remember what you see, for a large specimen can kill several people.

## IDENTIFICATION

The cap is 1¼–6 in across. It is quite round at first, flattening with age. It has a smooth, almost shiny surface. The color is often greenish turning to a rather dirty brown, but beware, in wet weather the cap can become quite pale. The stem is 2–5 in and white. The gills are free and quite crowded; white at first, mature specimens may have an almost flesh-colored tinge. The flesh is white with a yellow tinge by the cap, and it smells quite sweet. The volval sac or cup is quite pronounced. The spore print is white.

## HABITAT AND SEASON

Widespread in mixed deciduous woodland, particularly in association with oak. The season is early summer to late autumn.

The death cap deserves its name, it is the most deadly fungus known to mankind and years of research have not produced any antidote to the

*white unchanging gills*

*olive cap may sometimes be white or yellowish*

*white, cup-like volva surrounds stem base*

**RIGHT** *The caps often have a slightly radially streaked or fibrous appearance.*

poison. Many have tried and some people have been saved by having their blood screened through charcoal, once the hospital had identified it as *Amanita* poisoning. The symptoms of poisoning take between 10 and 24 hours to become apparent, but during that time the poison has been attacking the liver and the kidneys. The first signs of poisoning are prolonged sickness and diarrhoea with severe abdominal pains; this is often followed by a period of apparent recovery when all seems well. However, death from liver and kidney failure will occur within a few days. There is a rare form of *A. phalloides* which is *A. phalloides* var. *alba*. Apart from being pure white throughout, which makes it look deceptively like an innocent mushroom, the features by which you will identify it are exactly the same and it is just as deadly.

**ABOVE** *The volva at the stem base may be completely hidden under the leaf litter, as seen here – beware!*

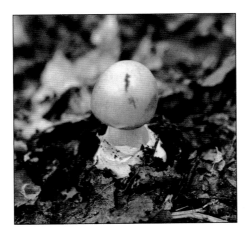

**LEFT** *Always carefully clear away around the stem base to expose the remains of a volva.*

## *Amanita virosa*
# DESTROYING ANGEL

Like many *Amanitas*, the destroying angel grows from a volval cup. It is deadly poisonous and well deserves its name, being white and fatal. The symptoms of the poison are the same as for *Amanita phalloides*.

### IDENTIFICATION
The cap is 2–6 in across, bell-shaped at first, it becomes very irregular when open. It is pure white. The stem is 3½–4¾ in and grows from a fairly large volval cup that is not regular at the base, but can clearly be seen with the fungus growing from it. There is a white ring which is very fragile and often incomplete. The gills are pure white. The flesh is white and the smell is slightly sickly. The spore print is white.

### HABITAT AND SEASON
Grows in mixed deciduous woodland and is happily not as common as the death cap. The season is usually midsummer to autumn. If you are on a foray, this is another mushroom that you should ask the leader to point out to you, for once seen you will be unlikely to forget it.

*slightly pointed cap*

*large, white cup-like volva*

**RIGHT** *The cap of this species often has a distinct hump or blunt point at the center.*

## Clitocybe dealbata

Do not be fooled by this innocent-looking little mushroom, it is severely toxic. It often grows in just the places that many edible mushrooms grow (*n.b. Marasmius oreades*).

### IDENTIFICATION

The cap is ¾–2 in across, flat with a depression slightly inrolled and fluted round the edge. It is off-white in color. The stem is ¾–1¼ in and whitish. The gills are quite crowded and run part way down the stem. They are almost cream in color. The flesh is white and it has a mealy smell. The spore print is white.

### HABITAT AND SEASON

Grows in lawns, pastures and old meadows, often in groups or rings. It can be also be found in open woodland. The season is summer to late autumn and it is quite common.

gills run down
the stem
(decurrent)

silky or
frosted appearance
of cap surface

## Clitocybe rivulosa

Another innocent-looking, but severely toxic mushroom that can easily be confused with the edible fairy ring mushroom, *Marasmius oreades*. Both grow in rings, in similar sites and at much the same time of the year. Indeed it is not uncommon for rings of each species to grow within a few yards of each other. So take care. It would probably be a good idea to seek out live examples of both before you start picking the fairy ring mushroom.

**BELOW** Clitocybe rivulosa *mushrooms are usually a silky grayish-white, as here.*

smooth silky cap

gills run down the stem

although the gills are buff the spores are white.

slightly funnel-shaped cap

gills are crowded

## HABITAT AND SEASON

In groups or rings in sandy soil amongst grass, beside paths and roads. The season is late summer to late autumn and it is very common.

**BELOW** *These caps are rather waterlogged and so appear browner than normal. Usually they are a silky grayish-white.*

## IDENTIFICATION

The cap is ¾–2 in across; cup-shaped at first, it soon flattens out with a small depression in the center. The margin remains slightly rolled. It is gray and concentric rings are visible. The stem is ¾–1½ in and a similar color to the cap. The crowded, gray gills run part way down the stem. The flesh is dirty white to gray. The closeness of the gills and the color and shape of the cap are important ways to distinguish this mushroom from the fairy ring mushroom. The spore print is white.

## *Coprinus atramentarius*
# COMMON INK CAP

The common ink cap or alcohol ink cap is not poisonous in itself, but if eaten in conjunction with alcohol, it can cause alarming symptoms, such as nausea, palpitations and stomach cramps. For this reason it has been used over the years in attempts to cure alcoholics. The ink cap gets its name from the fact that it was used many years ago by monks to produce an exceptionally fine drawing ink, made by boiling the collapsed inky caps with a little water and a hint of cloves. The difference between the common ink cap and the shaggy ink cap is quite marked, but it is important that you recognize this one for it would be a catastrophe to make a mistake at a party at which you were serving alcohol. Young specimens of the magpie fungus, *Coprinus picaceus*, could be confused with the common ink cap. Although not as common as this, it grows in fairly large quantities in the late summer to autumn. It is best avoided because although not poisonous, it can cause nausea and vomiting in some people.

### IDENTIFICATION
The cap is ¾–1½ in across, white and bell-shaped. Light gray to grayish-brown in color, with veil remnants often attached to the cap. The stem is 2¾–6¾ in and white. The gills are crowded, white at first, they change from brown to a dark inky mass. The smell is not distinctive. The spore print is brown.

### HABITAT AND SEASON
The common ink cap grows in tufts, often in association with buried wood. The season is from spring to late autumn and they are very common, often growing in large groups.

*gills blacken and liquify when mature from the edge inwards*

*note brown scaly base to stem*

**LEFT** *This is one of the most common species in towns, gardens and woodlands everywhere, often associated with dead or buried wood.*

## *Galerina autumnalis*
# DEADLY GALERINA

This fungus is deadly poisonous and must be avoided. The poisoning is very similar to that of the *Amanita* family.

### IDENTIFICATION

The cap is 1–2¾ in across. It is convex at first, becoming flat with a slight dome at the center. It is a dark brown fading to a light buff with age, and when moist is quite sticky and shiny. The hollow stem is ¾–4 in and fairly bulbous at the base. There are slight brownish to blackish markings at the base of the stem, and the mycelial threads are clearly visible at the bottom. There is a veil that breaks fairly easily and is quite small. The gills are attached and quite close, yellowish in color, becoming redder with age. The flesh is off-white. The deadly galerina has no smell. The spore print of the deadly galerina is dull orange-brown.

### HABITAT AND SEASON

The deadly galerina tends to live on well-decayed coniferous or deciduous wood, often in quite large groups. Its season is from late spring to autumn through winter, depending on the zone. The deadly galerina is not known in Europe, but common in North America. The very similar *G. marginata*, however, is common in Britain and is equally deadly.

**ABOVE** *Note the brownish-yellow gills which distinguish this from edible species such as the honey mushroom. The gills of the honey mushroom often darken in age, but they always have white spores.*

## *Hygrophoropsis aurantiaca*
# FALSE CHANTERELLE

Although not poisonous in the way that agaric and amanita mushrooms are, the false chanterelle is known to cause gastrointestinal problems.

**IDENTIFICATION**

The cap is ¾–3 in across, flat at first with a slightly inrolled margin, it becomes more funnel-shaped with age. In large specimens the cap is more fluted and looks much more like a chanterelle. However, the false chanterelle's cap is orange rather than the yellow of the true chanterelle. The gills are dark orange, close and run down the stem. The spore print is white.

**ABOVE AND RIGHT** *The false chanterelle is very common under both pine and birch trees, and the cap becomes funnel-shaped with age.*

*crowded gills are soft and often forked*

*cap margin inrolled when young*

**HABITAT AND SEASON**

Grows in coniferous woodland and on scrubland. It is very common and often grows in groups close to chanterelles. The season is from summer to late autumn.

## *Hypholoma fasciculare*
# SULPHUR TUFT

This is a very common mushroom and grows all the year round, even in the winter. It is not deadly poisonous, but definitely should be avoided. It could be confused with other fungi, such as honey mushrooms, *Armillaria mellea*, and brick cap, *Hypholoma sublateritium*, that are extremely good to eat, so take care with your identification.

### IDENTIFICATION

The cap is ¾–3½ in across and is convex. The remains of the yellow veil often adhere to the margin. The cap itself is bright yellow with a dark orange center. The stem is 1½–4 in, curved and a similar color to the cap. The gills are first bright yellow, but turn dark sulphur-green, then brown with age. The flesh is bright yellow, becoming brownish near the base of the stem. It has quite a mushroomy smell. The spore print is purple-black.

### HABITAT AND SEASON

This occurs in dense clusters on the rotting timber and stumps of deciduous and coniferous trees. It grows throughout the year.

*note purple-brown spores deposited on stem*

**BELOW** *One of the most common fungi everywhere on dead or dying wood, the sulphur tuft grows in large clumps.*

*Inocybe patouillardii*
# RED-STAINING INOCYBE

The red-staining inocybe is severely toxic and therefore must not be eaten. Many of the others in this family are poisonous, if not as deadly as this one, therefore it is best to avoid all the inocybes.

## IDENTIFICATION
The cap is 1¼–4 in across, slightly conical and uneven. The margins are often cracked, giving the typical appearance of an inocybe. Cream-colored, the cap has red-staining fibres. The stem is 1¼–4 in, fairly thick and slightly bulbous at the base. The gills are quite pink at first, like those of a mushroom, and then darken to a light brown color. The flesh is white and has no particular smell. The spore print is dull brown.

## HABITAT AND SEASON
Grows along paths in mixed woodland on chalky soils, especially those with beech and, less often, chestnut. The season is spring to late autumn.

**RIGHT** *The white fibrous cap and stem, with blood-red stains when bruised, are very distinctive. The red-staining inocybe likes open woodlands on alkaline soils.*

## Lactarius pubescens

*Lactarius pubescens* is a member of the large milk cap family. It is important to be able to identify this mushroom for not only is it a strong emetic but it can be confused with the edible saffron milk-cap *Lactarius deliciosus*. The woolly edges of *Lactarius pubescens* are an important feature of identification.

### IDENTIFICATION

The cap is 1½–4 in across, convex and slightly depressed with the margin markedly inrolled and woolly at the edge. It is often quite pale to rose pink; but this tends to fade in direct sunlight. The stem is 1¼–2½ in and a palish pink. The gills are crowded, light pink and tend to darken with age. They run down the stem. The flesh is quite thick and whitish, but can have a pinkish tinge. There is no particular smell. Equally common and shaggy is *L. torminosus*, a brigh-

**BELOW** *The cap should be pale pinkish-white, if the caps are deep pink you may have* Lactarius torminosus.

ter pink and equally upsetting if eaten. The spore print is creamy-white.

### HABITAT AND SEASON

This mushroom tends to grow fairly widely but often near birch trees on fairly poor or sandy soil. The season is from late summer through to late autumn.

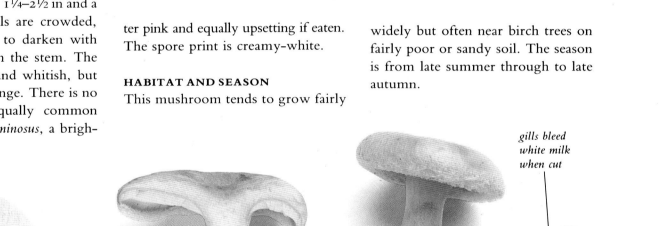

*gills bleed white milk when cut*

*funnel-shaped cap*

*Paxillus involutus*
# POISON PAXILLUS

**ABOVE** *A mature cap with margin unrolled.*

The poison paxillus is a very common mushroom. It is also severely toxic. It can have a bolete-like shape, which makes matters worse, some bolete species being, of course, edible. The toxins have yet to be identified, but their effect is somewhat similar to leukemia.

### IDENTIFICATION

The cap size is 2–6 in across. It is quite flat when young, becoming convex and somewhat funnel-shaped with age. It gets its name from its clearly inrolled rim. This color is mid- to red-brown. The cap is slippery when moist and shiny when dry. The stem is up to 3 in and similar in color to the cap. The narrow, crowded gills are yellow turning brown to red-brown when bruised. The gills run down the stem. The spore print is sienna.

### HABITAT AND SEASON

The poison paxillus grows beside paths in broad-leaved woodland, especially with birch, and on quite acid scrubland. It has a long growing season from summer to late autumn.

**ABOVE** *This is an immature cap with tightly rolled cap margin.*

crowded
gills
bruise brown

inrolled
margin

## *Russula emetica*
# THE SICKENER

There are at least 150 different species of *Russula*, making it one of the largest groups of fungi. Some, such as the charcoal burner, are edible, but many are highly poisonous. The sickener and the very similar looking beechwood sickener, *Russula mairei*, did not get their names without good reason. It is really best to leave this family well alone.

### IDENTIFICATION

The cap is 1¼–4 in across and is cup-shaped, later flattening with a shallow central depression. The cap is a brightish red, but sometimes has faded white areas. When peeled, it shows red-colored flesh underneath. The white stem is 1½–3½ in. The gills are creamy, darkening slightly with age. The flesh is thin and fragile and can be quite sticky. It is white except under the cap. The smell is sweet and fruity. The spore print is whitish.

**BELOW** *The sickener is found under pines, especially in wet areas.*

### HABITAT AND SEASON

Grows almost exclusively under pines. The season is summer to late autumn and it is very common. As its name suggests, the beechwood sickener, which has a similar season, grows almost exclusively under beech trees.

*pure red cap skin peels off very easily*

*flesh is brittle and crumbly*

*widely spaced gills*

# Cooking with Mushrooms

# INTRODUCTION

From the cook's point of view, wild mushrooms are an irresistible source of flavor, texture and aroma. The recipes in this book explore the qualities of over thirty types of edible mushrooms and will show you how best to cook and enjoy them.

The passions associated with picking mushrooms are easily aroused when we realize how many good mushrooms there are growing freely in our woods and fields. Coupled with the excitement of picking mushrooms in the wild is the risk of handling poisonous varieties, such as the death cap *Amanita phalloides*, panther cap *Amanita pantherina*, yellow stainer *Agaricus xanthodermus* and destroying angel *Amanita virosa*. These often deadly poisonous mushrooms can easily be mistaken for the common and edible field mushroom *Agaricus campestris*. For your own safety, never touch a mushroom you cannot identify. When possible, accompany someone who knows which mushrooms are safe, and remember, if in doubt, don't touch them.

There are over a thousand varieties of mushroom known to be edible. The mushrooms which are best to eat are a question of taste, but it is generally agreed that the finest include the cep *Boletus edulis*, bay bolete *Boletus badius*, morel *Morchella esculenta*, chanterelle *Cantherellus cibarius* and chicken of the woods *Laetiporus sulphureus*. These mushrooms fetch a high price in the market and are sold mainly to the restaurant trade. Occasionally you may find them for sale in specialty food stores. Most precious of all is the fresh truffle which is found mainly in northern Italy and southern parts of France. Black and white truffles are found beneath the soil in mature woodland and are prized for their mysterious scent

which, it is said, imitates the pheromone that causes pigs to mate.

The scent of wild mushrooms in damp woodland is enough to get most people on their knees scratching through the undergrowth. You may not be lucky enough to find a truffle, but there are many fine mushrooms to find and a home-cooked breakfast is a welcome return for the hungry mushroom picker. Even if you've only managed to find a few mushrooms, they will go a long way to flavor a plate of scrambled eggs. Parsley, thyme and fennel-scented chervil bring out their flavor as will a splash of sherry. Later in the day, wild mushrooms are ideal cooked in warming soups and broths. More delicate mushrooms are better suited to light broths.

Poultry and game taste good with mushroom flavors, either roasted, braised or sautéed. When cooking free-range chicken, try the delicate richness of the chanterelle, saffron milk-cap *Lactarius deliciosus*, hedgehog fungus *Hydnum repandum* and honey mushroom *Armillaria mellea*. Guinea fowl and pheasant carry the robust flavor of the fresh or dried cep, bay bolete, parasol mushroom and blewit. Wild duck mirrors the smoky richness of the morel and is good served with a glass of Madeira. Chicken of the woods has such a convincing taste, texture and appearance that it can be used as a substitute for chicken in chicken recipes.

Beef is a perfect match for the large field, horse and parasol mushroom. Cooked slowly with red wine, onions and a good stock, they are the making of a fine beef stew, rich and round with a luscious mushroom gravy. The delicate quality of lamb allies with the apricot sweetness of the chanterelle and saffron milk-cap.

Pork belongs in a slow pot with a sauce of Jerusalem artichokes, horn of plenty *Craterellus cornucopiodes* and a purée of green olives.

The flavor of wild mushrooms is most effective with other wild foods. The sea is perhaps the most bountiful source of wild food, both fish and shellfish. Providing they are fresh (and in some cases alive), fish and shellfish are ideal ingredients to accompany wild mushrooms. When you have chosen the finest ingredients, simplicity is the best course of action, with particular care given to the preparation of sauces and garnishes. As a rule, if the fish has a delicate flavor, select a sweeter, subtle-tasting mushroom. Flat fish, such as sole, flounder and halibut suit field varieties, with a little parsley, lemon and thyme. Stronger oily fish such as salmon, tuna and trout benefit from the assertive quality of the cep, bay bolete, shiitake and blewit mushrooms.

Wild mushrooms have been valued for centuries as an alternative to meat; a delight for those who know how and where to pick them. Meat has always been expensive in the market and mushrooms have long been used to make it go further. Presently, with eating habits veering away from meat for health reasons, vegetarians are discovering again the value of wild mushrooms for their first-rate flavor and goodness. Mushrooms contain essential minerals, potassium, magnesium and iron. They are high in niacin and contain other B group vitamins. Mushrooms consist of 2–8% protein and contain around 35 calories per 4 oz. A section of this book has purely vegetarian recipes, while many recipes in the breakfast and starter sections will also appeal to vegetarians.

# GOOD EDIBLE MUSHROOMS

*Amanita caesarea*
**Caesar's mushroom**

*Boletus edulis*
**Cep**

*Armillaria mellea*
**Honey fungus**

*Cantharellus cibarius*
**Chanterelle**

*Agaricus campestris* and *bisporus*
**Field mushroom**

*Boletus badius*
**Bay boletus**

*Calocybe gambosa*
**St George's mushroom**

The assessment and value of edible mushrooms is open to opinion. Apart from the principle of putting delicate mushrooms with subtle foods and not putting mushrooms that stain black in creamy sauces, there are no rules to follow. Below is a brief and personal assessment of good edible mushrooms.

### *Agaricus campestris* and *bisporus*
### Field Mushroom
Open and closed field mushrooms provide a well-known flavour to everyday cooking. Take care when picking not to confuse this common mushroom with the poisonous yellow stainer *Agaricus xanthodermus*, destroying angel *Amanita virosa* and spring amanita *Amanita verna*.

### *Amanita caesarea*
### Caesar's Mushroom
The Caesar's mushroom is valued for

its sweet chestnut quality. It has a russet orange to yellow glow. It is not found in Britain. Young specimens are best eaten raw in salads.

### *Armillaria mellea*
### Honey Fungus or Boot-lace Fungus
This fungus has a strong, often astringent, smell. It is edible only after blanching in water which must be discarded. However, after blanching, honey fungus softens and loses much of its appeal. It is an acquired taste.

### *Boletus badius*
### Bay Boletus
The bay boletus shares many qualities with the cep. Young specimens are particularly good and offer a lingering richness to be enjoyed raw in salads or cooked simply to respect their flavour.

### *Boletus edulis*
### Cep or Penny Bun
The cep is considered best when small and tight. Good specimens are heavy for their size and have an almost leafy, richness when eaten raw. Larger ceps are best cooked in butter with a few herbs. Another bolete which is popular and looks like the cep is *Boletus pruinatus*.

### *Calocybe gambosa*
### St George's Mushroom
The St George's mushroom has a rich meaty scent and a nutty flavour when cooked. They are good eaten raw or with a touch of garlic and a few chives in an olive oil dressing.

### *Cantharellus cibarius*
### Chanterelle
The intensely orange trumpet shape of the chanterelle has an appealing scent of dried apricots with a hint of

*Craterellus cornucopiodes*
**Horn of plenty**

*Coprinus comatus*
**Shaggy ink cap**

*Hydnum repandum*
**Hedgehog fungus**

*Flammulina velutipes*
**Enokitake**

*Laccaria amethystea*
**Amethyst deceiver**

*Cantharellus infundibuliformis*
**Winter Chanterelle**

*Lactarius deliciosus*
**Saffron milk-cap**

citrus. Chanterelle are best tossed in nut brown butter, although their colour and flavour remain true even after slow cooking. It is essential to avoid the false chanterelle *Hygrophoropsis aurantiaca* which can cause alarming hallucinations.

*Cantharellus infundibuliformis*
## Winter Chanterelle
This mushroom has a rich mossy scent that combines well with other mushrooms. After trimming at the base, the winter chanterelle is best used whole.

*Coprinus comatus*
## Shaggy Ink Cap or Lawyer's Wig
The shaggy ink cap has a delicate flavour not unlike the field mushroom. Pick young specimens that have yet to blacken and deteriorate around the fringe. Use in smooth soups and sauces. Do not use the common ink cap *Coprinus atramentarius*; this causes a violent reaction when consumed with alcohol.

*Craterellus cornucopiodes*
## Horn of Plenty or Trompette des Morts
The horn of plenty has a sweet earthy richness that goes a long way to flavour soups, stews and casseroles. Its jet black appearance does not bleed, even after lengthy cooking.

*Flammulina velutipes*
## Enokitake
These long-stemmed pinhead mushrooms are grown commercially on the stumps of the enoki or Chinese hackberry tree. They have a delicate flavour reminiscent of white pepper and lemon. Serve them raw or cooked in a light broth. Enokitake are available in Oriental grocers.

*Hydnum repandum*
## Hedgehog Fungus or Pied de Mouton
Young hedgehog fungus has a peppery watercress quality that is appreciated raw in salads. Mature specimens can be bitter and are best cooked with sweet butter and herbs.

*Laccaria amethystea*
## Amethyst Deceiver
These distinctive grape coloured mushrooms have a subtle, gentle flavour, but provide colour and interest when put with paler mushrooms.

*Lactarius deliciosus*
## Saffron Milk-cap
The saffron milk-cap is prized for its saffron orange colour and firm texture. It has little flavour. Mature specimens often harbour insect larvae in the stem and centre cap, so take care when selecting.

*Laetiporus sulphureus*
**Chicken of the woods**

*Leccinum versipelle*
**Orange birch bolete**

*Marasmius oreades*
**Fairy ring mushroom**

*Langermannia gigantea*
**Giant puffball**

*Macrolepiota procera*
**Parasol mushroom**

*Lentinus edodes*
**Shiitake**

*Lepista nuda*
**Wood blewit**

*Lepista saeva*
**Field blewit**

*Morchella esculenta, vulgaris*
and *elata*
**Morels**

*Langermannia gigantea*
## Giant Puffball
When sliced open, the young giant puffball has a gentle meaty rich aroma similar in some ways to the cep. Older specimens discolor yellow when cut and should not be eaten.

*Leccinum versipelle*
## Orange Birch Bolete
It has a mud spattered stem and a tawny orange cap which fades with age. It softens when cooked and provides a good texture for casseroles.

*Lentinus edodes*
## Shiitake
Shiitake are grown commercially in the Far East on logs that are taken from the oak related *shii* tree. They have a robust beefy sweetness that remains even after lengthy cooking.

*Lepista nuda* (syn. *Tricholoma nuda*) and *Lepista saeva*
## Blewit and Field Blewit
Both blewits have an assertive pine-rich perfume, that belongs with the pronounced flavor of game, toasted nuts and cheeses.

*Macrolepiota procera*
## Parasol Mushroom
This handsome mushroom stands proudly on a tough inedible stem. Its cap offers a gamey rich flavor which strengthens when mature. Parasol mushrooms are best sautéed in butter with a few fresh herbs.

*Marasmius oreades*
## Fairy Ring Mushroom
Fresh and dried, this common mushroom has an oaky scent which is best cooked simply in sweet butter. Great care should be taken not to confuse the fairy ring mushroom with the deadly poisonous *Clitocybe rivulosa* and *Clitocybe dealbata*.

*Morchella esculenta, vulgaris* and *elata*
## Morels
The morels are the most exciting springtime fungi. Both fresh and dried morels are prized for their tobacco-rich scent of sulphur and oak. This curious scent combines especially well with eggs, beef and game. A splash of Madeira will enhance their flavor.

*Pleurotus citrinopileatus*
## Yellow Oyster Mushroom
This pretty mushroom is designed by the mushroom cultivator to capture our attention in the supermarket.

*Pleurotus ostreatus*
**Oyster mushroom**

*Pleurotus citrinopileatus*
**Yellow oyster mushroom**

*Suillus luteus*
**Slippery jack**

*Tuber magnatum*
**White truffle**

*Russula cyanoxantha*
**Charcoal burner**

*Sparassis crispa*
**Cauliflower fungus**

*Tuber aestivum*
**Summer truffle**

However, it tastes of very little and its color disappears when cooked.

### *Pleurotus ostreatus*
### Oyster Mushroom
Both wild and cultivated oyster mushrooms have little flavor or aroma. Young specimens are best and provide bulk when combining with stronger-flavored mushrooms.

### *Russula cyanoxantha*
### Charcoal Burner
The charcoal burner is an excellent mushroom to eat. However, it is a member of a very large genus and identification can be very difficult. Correct identification is essential because some are poisonous.

### *Sparassis crispa*
### Cauliflower Fungus
The cauliflower fungus is known more for its texture than its flavor.

When raw and dried it has a curious scent of latex and ammonia which goes after brief cooking. The crisp texture is appreciated when combined with other mushrooms.

### *Suillus luteus* (syn. *Boletus luteus*)
### Slippery Jack or Pine Bolete
The slippery jack, so named because of its gluten covered cap, tends to absorb moisture in wet weather. When cooked, it softens to provide a basis for smooth soups and sauces.

### *Tricholoma ponderosa*
### White Matsutake
Not known in Europe, it is common in North America. It has an interesting flavor.

### *Tuber aestivum*
### Summer Truffle
Less intensely flavored than the white truffle, this warty black variety has a

more delicate aroma associated with oak woodlands rather than the farm. More robust in texture than its white counterpart, the summer truffle should be pared before slicing raw. Truffles benefit from a few drops of truffle oil added towards the end of cooking.

### *Tuber magnatum*
### Piedmont or White Truffle
This rare and expensive tuber is found in very limited areas, mostly in northern Italy. It has a strong and curious aroma connected with the intensity of a pig sty! To touch, the white truffle has the fragility of firm fresh yeast. Unfortunately highly trained dogs or pigs are needed to find it. If you are fortunate enough to come by a white truffle, scrub it clean and shave over plainly cooked food. The flavor of the white truffle goes if it is cooked.

## Drying Mushrooms

The process of drying mushrooms intensifies individual flavors and aromas. The cep develops a pronounced beefy, rich aroma with a chamois leather sweetness. The bay boletes have a more pronounced sweetness and a less complex aroma. The morel develops a sulphur-rich, beefy, almost smoky quality, while fairy rings have a gentle sweetness. The cauliflower fungus has a strong latex vinegar smell which disappears with cooking. The saffron milk-cap and chanterelle have a fruity richness and the horn of plenty has a dark sweet woodland flavor.

When fully dried, mushrooms will keep through the winter in air-tight jars, providing a useful and nutritious source of flavor for soups, stews and casseroles.

*1* To make sure the mushrooms are free from infestation, wipe them with a damp cloth, but avoid washing, and cut away damaged parts. Slice the mushrooms thinly. When drying chanterelles, remove the stems of small specimens as they tend to toughen.

*3* *(Right)* When mushrooms are completely dry, place each variety in an air-tight jar, label and store in a dark place. If mushrooms are not fully dry before storing, molds will grow and spoil your work.

*2* Lay the mushrooms on a basket tray, or baking sheet lined with several layers of newspaper and a final layer of baking parchment. Put in a warm and well-ventilated place for two days. For fast drying, preheat an oven with fan to 150°F, keep the door ajar and dry the mushrooms for 2 hours. If you have a small quantity of mushrooms, thread them with needle and thread and hang up to dry.

## Mushroom Powder

The intense flavor of dried mushrooms can be used in powder form to enliven winter soups, stews and curries. The curry-scented milk-cap, *Lactarius camphoratus*, offers a pungent reminder of fenugreek and should always be used sparingly. The anise mushroom, *Clitocybe odora* is another powerful substitute for spices and can be used in sweet and savory cooking. Other mushrooms suitable for powdering include many of the boletes and field and horse mushrooms.

## To Reconstitute Dried Mushrooms

To bring dried mushrooms back to life, they need to be soaked in warm water for 20 minutes. Boiling water will make them tough. The water used to soak dried mushrooms should be saved and added to stocks.

*1* Wipe clean the inside of a coffee grinder with a dry cloth. Put in the well-dried mushrooms and reduce to a fine powder.

*2* Transfer to an air-tight jar, label and keep in a dark place. Use sparingly.

*1* Place the mushrooms in a bowl. Cover with warm water and let stand for 20 minutes.

## Salt Preserving

Salt preserving is an age-old method of keeping mushrooms, and is still used in countries of the former Soviet Union. The method eliminates bacterial growth by packing mushrooms with layers of salt. The salt draws out the moisture in the mushrooms, forming a brine. Before using, the mushrooms need to be soaked in plenty of cold water to reduce saltiness. After soaking, salt preserved mushrooms can be added to braised meats such as beef, pork and tripe.

Suitable mushrooms for salting include: hedgehog fungus, oyster mushroom, bay bolete, winter chanterelle, saffron milk-cap and wood blewit.

The proportion of salt to mushrooms is 3–1.

*1* *(Right)* Wipe the mushrooms clean with a damp cloth, trim and ensure that they are free from grit and infestation. Slice the mushrooms thickly with a stainless steel knife. Place a layer of rock or sea salt in the bottom of a covered glass or stoneware jar, layer with mushrooms. Alternate with more salt and mushrooms until full.

*2* After 3–4 hours, you will find the volume of mushrooms will drop as the salt draws out their moisture. At this stage additional layers of salt and mushrooms can be added. Salted mushrooms will keep safely in a cool place for up to 12 months.

## Freezing Mushrooms

To preserve mushrooms quickly and effectively, consider freezing them. Firmer varieties are best, such as shiitake, blewits, horn of plenty, chanterelle, closed field and horse mushrooms. To thaw, take Antonio Carluccio's advice and immerse briefly in boiling water before using.

*1* Bring a saucepan of salted water to the boil and line a tray with greaseproof paper. Ensure mushrooms are free from grit and infestation then trim and slice thickly if large. Drop the mushrooms into the boiling water and simmer for 1 minute.

*2* Drain well and open freeze for 30–40 minutes on a paper-lined tray. When frozen, turn loosely into plastic bags, label and return to the freezer for up to 6 months.

## Preserving Mushrooms in Butter

Capturing the flavor and aroma of wild mushrooms in butter is a favorite method of preserving. The finest *Boletus*, *B. edulis*, *B. badius* and *B. pruinatus*, retain their qualities best when softened and combined with unsalted butter. If you are lucky enough to chance upon a few fresh truffles, these also keep well, peeled, chopped and concealed raw in butter. Other mushrooms that keep well in butter include the morel, chanterelle, saffron milk-cap and Caesar's mushroom. Wild mushroom butter is delicious melted over simply cooked meat or fish. It is also good over pasta, or in soups, sauces and gravies.

| |
|---|
| *1 lb / 4½ cups mushrooms* |
| *¾ cup unsalted butter* |
| *½ oz / ½ cup fresh black or white truffle, peeled and chopped (optional), or 3 drops truffle oil (optional)* |

*1* Be sure the mushrooms are free from grit and infestation. Trim, slice and chop. Melt 2 oz / 4 tbsp of the butter in a large nonstick frying pan. Add the mushrooms and sauté over a gentle heat to reduce the volume, then simmer in their own juices for 2–3 minutes. Cool.

*3* *(Right)* Roll into a cigar shape, twist each end and label. Refrigerate for up to 10 days or freeze for up to 8 weeks.

*2* Combine the cooked mushrooms and truffles, or oil if you are using this instead, with the remaining butter and spoon the mixture onto a square of greaseproof paper.

## Duxelle

Duxelle is a preparation known in classical French cooking. It consists of finely chopped mushrooms and shallots cooked in butter, wine and herbs, and forms the basis for many well-known soups, sauces, stuffings, gratins and fillings. The name, according to Larousse, derives from a small town in the north east of France called Uxel. The preparation may be credited to La Varenne who cooked for the household of the Marquis d'Uxelles in the 17th century. Duxelle can be made from wild or cultivated mushrooms and refrigerated or frozen in ice cube portions for 10 days or 8 weeks respectively.

| |
|---|
| *4 tbsp unsalted butter* |
| *2 shallots, chopped* |
| *1 lb / 4½ cups wild and/or cultivated mushrooms, trimmed and finely chopped* |
| *1 sprig thyme, chopped* |
| *3½ tbsp white wine or sherry* |
| *celery salt* |
| *freshly ground black pepper* |

*2* *(Right)* Add the mushrooms, thyme and wine and simmer so that the mushroom juices run, then increase the heat to boil off the moisture. When quite dry, season with celery salt and pepper, if using right away. Otherwise, cool and refrigerate or freeze.

*1* Melt the butter in a large nonstick frying pan over a gentle heat, add the shallots and sauté for 2–3 minutes to soften without browning.

## Mushroom Purée

Mushroom purée takes Duxelle a stage further and reduces it to a fine purée. Mushroom purée is used mainly for the enrichment of soups and sauces, although a spoonful works wonders in a casserole of beef or game. As with the Duxelle, mushroom purée freezes conveniently in ice cube portions.

*1* Prepare the Duxelle as shown in the previous recipe. Spoon into a food processor and blend until smooth.

*2* Allow to cool, transfer into an airtight jar and refrigerate for up to 10 days or freeze for up to 8 weeks.

## Mushroom Extract

The finest edible mushrooms are best preserved whole or sliced. More common although less elegant species such as the field, horse and parasol mushroom lend their flavor and color to a dark extract. It is very important to ensure mushrooms are properly identified before using. An incorrectly identified mushroom put among the others can cause fatal illness. Shaggy ink caps are worth putting in, as are any overgrown boletus mushrooms providing they are free from infestation and are in good condition. Any deterioration can cause the extract to ferment at a later date. The flavor extracted from the mushrooms will keep in the refrigerater in a screw-top jar or bottle for 8–10 weeks. Use readily to enliven and enrich winter soups, stews and game dishes.

*1* Place all the ingredients in a large stainless steel pan. Bring to a boil and simmer uncovered for 45 minutes.

*2* Strain the mushrooms through a fine mesh strainer, pressing as much liquid as possible back into the pan. Return the extract to the boil and reduce to half its volume.

| 1 lb / 4½ cups field, horse and parasol mushrooms, shaggy ink caps, honey mushrooms, slippery jack and/or winter chanterelles, trimmed and roughly chopped |
| --- |
| 1¼ cups water |
| ⅞ cup red wine |
| 4 tbsp dark soy sauce |
| 1 tsp salt |
| 1 sprig thyme |

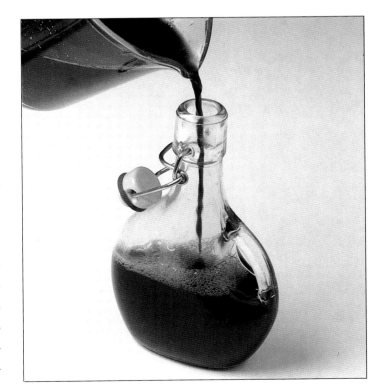

*3* *(Left)* Sterilize a preserving jar or bottle by immersing it in boiling water for a few minutes. Drain. Fill the jar or bottle with the mushroom liquid, cover and allow to cool. When cool, label and store in the refrigerator. Mushroom extract can be frozen and used in ice cube portions.

## Pickled Mushrooms

The principle of pickling eliminates the chance of bacterial growth by immersing mushrooms in vinegar. Vinegar can be flavored and diluted to lessen the sharp taste. In this recipe shiitake mushrooms take on an oriental flavor, although other firm mushrooms and spices can also be used. It is best to dress pickled mushrooms with olive oil when serving, to restore balance. Serve as an appetizer or buffet style lunch item.

| |
| --- |
| 1 cup white wine vinegar |
| 2/3 cup water |
| 1 tsp salt |
| 1 red chili |
| 2 tsp coriander seeds |
| 2 tsp szechuan pepper or anise-pepper |
| 9 oz / 3 cups shiitake mushrooms, halved if large |

*1* Bring the wine vinegar and water to a simmer in a stainless steel pan. Add the salt, chili, coriander, szechuan pepper or anise-pepper and mushrooms and cook for 10 minutes.

*2* Sterilize a 2¼ cup preserving jar by immersing in boiling water. Drain until dry. Transfer mushrooms and liquid to the jar, seal, label and leave for at least 10 days before trying.

## Chanterelle Vodka

If you manage to find a few chanterelles on your mushroom foray, consider steeping them in vodka. Vodka has a neutral flavor and allows the apricot quality of the chanterelles to shine. Chill thoroughly before serving as an aperitif.

| |
| --- |
| 1½ cups vodka |
| 3 oz / 1 cup young chanterelle mushrooms, trimmed |

*1* Place the chanterelle mushrooms in a clean preserving bottle or jar.

*2* Pour in the vodka, cover and leave at room temperature. Chanterelle vodka is ready when the mushrooms have dropped to the bottom.

## Preserving Mushrooms in Oil

The method of preserving in oil is ideally suited to good quality firm mushrooms. The process can seem expensive, but the oil used takes on a delicious mushroom flavor which can then be used to make special salad dressings.

| |
| --- |
| *1 cup white wine vinegar* |
| *⅔ cup water* |
| *1 tsp salt* |
| *1 sprig thyme* |
| *½ bay leaf* |
| *1 red chili (optional)* |
| *1 lb / 4½ cups assorted wild mushrooms, including young bay bolete, chanterelles, saffron milk-caps and horn of plenty, trimmed and halved if large* |
| *1⅔ cups virgin olive oil* |

*1* Bring the vinegar and water to a simmer in a stainless steel pan. Add the salt, thyme, bay leaf and chili if using, and infuse for 15 minutes.

*2* Add the mushrooms and simmer for 10 minutes. Sterilize a 2¼ cup preserving jar by immersing in boiling water. Drain until dry. Lift the cooked mushrooms out of the liquid, drain well and place in the jar.

*3* (*Right*) Cover the mushrooms with oil, close the lid and label. Mushrooms in oil will keep in a cool place for up to 12 months.

## Spiced Mushrooms in Alcohol

Winter chanterelles and oyster mushrooms combine with caraway seeds, lemon and chili to make this unusual and warming infusion.

| |
| --- |
| *3 oz / 1 cup winter chanterelle and oyster mushrooms* |
| *1 tsp caraway seeds* |
| *1 lemon* |
| *1 red chili* |
| *1½ cups vodka* |

*1* Place the mushrooms, caraway seeds, lemon and chili in a clean preserving jar or bottle.

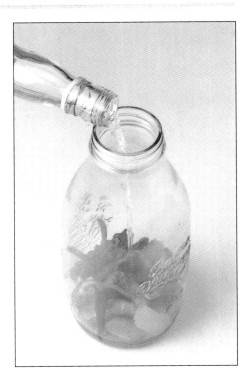

*2* Pour in the vodka and leave for 2–3 weeks until the mushrooms no longer float. Chill thoroughly and serve as an aperitif.

# Wild Mushroom Breakfasts

## Kedgeree of Oyster and Chanterelle Mushrooms

Providing breakfast for an army of late risers is quite a challenge. This delicious kedgeree combines the rich woodland flavor of oyster and chanterelle mushrooms with eggs, rice and a touch of curry seasoning.

### SERVES 4

| |
|---|
| 2 tbsp butter |
| 1 medium onion, chopped |
| 2 cups long grain rice |
| 1 small carrot, cut into julienne strips |
| 3¾ cups chicken or vegetable stock, boiling |
| 1 pinch saffron |
| 8 oz / 2½ cups oyster and chanterelle mushrooms, trimmed and halved |
| 4 oz floury potato, peeled and grated |
| 1⅞ cup milk |
| ½ chicken or vegetable stock cube |
| ½ tsp curry paste |
| 2 tbsp heavy cream |
| 4 eggs |
| 4 tbsp chopped fresh parsley |

**Cook's Tip**
Kedgeree will keep warm without spoiling in a covered dish for up to 2 hours.

*1* Melt the butter in a large saucepan, add the onion and fry it gently without letting it color.

*2* Turn half of the softened onion into a medium-sized saucepan. Put the rice, carrot and stock in the large pan, add a pinch of saffron, stir and simmer, uncovered for 15 minutes. Remove the pan from the heat, cover and stand for 5 minutes.

*3* Add the oyster and chanterelle mushrooms to the pan with the onion and cook gently for a few minutes to soften. Add the grated potato, milk, stock cube and curry paste and simmer for 15 minutes until the potatoes have thickened the liquid.

*4* Place the eggs in a pan of boiling water and cook for 10 minutes. Run them under cold water to cool, then peel and cut into quarters.

*5* Fork the rice onto a warmed serving platter. Spoon the mushrooms and sauce into the center and garnish with the egg quarters and chopped parsley.

**Cook's Tip**
There are many varieties of long grain rice available. The least flavorsome are the non-stick brands that have been part cooked to remove a proportion of starch. The notion that every grain of rice must be separate undermines the nature and flavor of good rice.

## Apricot Chanterelle Breakfast Muffins

Smell a chanterelle and you will be reminded of apricots. To encourage this association, here is a recipe for chanterelle muffins flecked with dried apricots and topped with pine nuts.

### MAKES 12

| |
|---|
| 1⅓ cups self-rising flour |
| ½ tsp salt |
| 1 tbsp chopped dried apricots |
| 3 oz / 1 cup chanterelle mushrooms, trimmed and chopped |
| 1 tsp chopped fresh thyme |
| 1 egg |
| 4 tbsp butter, melted |
| ½ cup milk |
| ¼ cup pine nuts or sliced almonds |
| melted butter or oil for brushing |

*1* Preheat the oven to 425°F. Grease 12 deep muffin tins with butter or oil and set aside.

*2* Sift the flour and salt into a bowl. Add the apricots, mushrooms, thyme, egg, butter and milk, then stir to make a thick batter.

*3* Spoon the mixture into the prepared muffin tins, so they are about two-thirds full. Sprinkle with pine nuts and bake near the top of the oven for 12 minutes until golden, then turn out and serve warm. They are particularly delicious cut in half and spread with butter.

## Egg, Bacon and Wild Mushroom Fry Up

When you arrive home tired and hungry after a mushroom hunt, a quick fry up will restore your strength and vitality.

### SERVES 4

| |
|---|
| 6 tbsp goose fat or lard |
| 12 oz bacon |
| 1 lb pork sausages |
| 12 oz / 3½ cups assorted wild mushrooms PALE: oyster and parasol mushrooms, hedgehog fungus, fairy ring and honey mushrooms, ceps, chanterelles and chicken of the woods. DARK: field mushrooms, shaggy ink caps, horn of plenty and queen boletes |
| 1 sprig thyme |
| salt and freshly ground black pepper |
| 4 eggs |
| 4 slices brown or white bread |
| butter for spreading |

*1* Preheat the oven to 300°F. Melt 2 tbsp of the fat in a large nonstick frying pan and fry the bacon and sausages. Transfer to a serving dish and keep warm.

### Cook's Tip
If using both pale and dark mushrooms, it is best to cook them separately, one batch at a time.

*2* Clean the mushrooms and slice if necessary. Add to the pan and toss in the fat, then add the thyme and cook for 2–3 minutes. Season with salt and pepper, transfer to a bowl, cover and keep warm.

*3* Melt the remaining fat in the pan and fry the eggs. Meanwhile toast the bread and spread with butter. Serve with the bacon, sausages and mushrooms.

## Toasted Brioche, Scrambled Eggs and Morels

Morels have a rich flavor that combines well with other rich ingredients such as eggs, cream and Madeira. This simple breakfast dish can be made with fresh or dried morels.

### SERVES 4

| |
|---|
| 5 oz / 1½ cups fresh morels or ½ oz / ¼ cup dried |
| 2 tbsp unsalted butter |
| 1 shallot, finely chopped |
| 4 tbsp Madeira |
| 4 tbsp crème fraîche |
| 4 small brioches |
| **For the Scrambled Eggs** |
| 8 eggs |
| 4 tbsp crème fraîche |
| salt and freshly ground black pepper |
| 2 tbsp unsalted butter |

*1* If using dried morels, cover with warm water, soak for 20 minutes and drain. Melt the butter in a non stick frying pan and gently fry the shallot until it is softened. Add the morels and cook briefly, then stir in the Madeira and cook until the liquid is syrupy. Stir in the crème fraîche and simmer briefly. Season, transfer to a bowl and keep warm.

*2* Remove the tops from the brioches and toast under a moderate broiler.

**Cook's Tip**
Madeira provides an oaky hazelnut flavor to balance stronger-tasting mushrooms. You can also use a medium dry sherry.

*3* Break the eggs into a bowl, add the crème fraîche, season and beat with a fork. Melt the butter in the frying pan, pour in the eggs and cook, stirring gently but continuously until the eggs are slightly cooked. Remove from the heat: the eggs will continue cooking in their own heat.

*4* Spoon the scrambled eggs over the brioches and top with morels.

## English Muffins with a Florentine Parasol Topping

The parasol mushroom is prized for its delicate texture and rich flavor. The stems of open specimens are tough but both the stem and cap of closed parasols are delicious with a creamy spinach topping.

### SERVES 4

| |
|---|
| 14 oz young leaf spinach, stems removed |
| salt and freshly ground black pepper |
| 12 oz / 3½ cups parasol mushroom caps |
| 4 tbsp unsalted butter, plus extra for spreading |
| ½ garlic clove, crushed |
| 5 sprigs thyme |
| 1 cup crème fraîche |
| pinch of grated nutmeg |
| 4 English muffins, split |

*1* Rinse the spinach in plenty of water, then place in a large saucepan with a pinch of salt. Cover and cook over a steady heat for 6–8 minutes, then drain in a colander, pressing out as much water as you can with the back of a spoon. Chop the spinach finely.

*2* Chop the mushrooms, with stems if small, very finely, then melt the butter in a frying pan and add the mushrooms together with the garlic and 1 sprig of thyme. Cook for 3–4 minutes then add the chopped spinach and ⅔ cup of the crème fraîche. Season with salt, pepper and a pinch of nutmeg. Toast the muffins, split and spread lightly with butter.

*3* Spoon the spinach mixture onto the muffins, top with the remaining crème fraîche and garnish with thyme.

**Cook's Tip**
If using frozen chopped spinach, allow half the weight of fresh spinach, defrost thoroughly and squeeze dry.

## Parsley, Lemon and Garlic Mushrooms on Toast

Field mushrooms have a long and happy relationship with garlic, but too often the intense flavor of the garlic takes over. With respect for the mushroom, the garlic in this recipe is tempered with a generous amount of fresh parsley and a touch of lemon.

### SERVES 4

| |
|---|
| *2 tbsp unsalted butter, plus extra for spreading* |
| *1 medium onion, chopped* |
| *1 garlic clove, crushed* |
| *12 oz / 3½ cups assorted wild mushrooms such as field mushrooms, shaggy ink caps and honey mushrooms, trimmed and sliced* |
| *3 tbsp dry sherry* |
| *5 tbsp chopped fresh parsley* |
| *1 tbsp lemon juice* |
| *salt and freshly ground black pepper* |
| *4 slices brown or white bread* |

**Cook's Tip**
Italian parsley has a good flavor and keeps well in the refrigerator. To keep it fresh, stand in a jar of water and cover with a plastic bag.

*1* Melt the butter in a large nonstick frying pan and gently sauté the onion without letting it color.

*3* Stir in the parsley and lemon juice, and then season to taste with salt and pepper.

*2* Add the garlic and mushrooms, cover and cook for 3–5 minutes. Add the sherry, cook uncovered to evaporate the liquid.

*4* Toast the bread and spread with butter. Spoon the mushrooms over the toast and serve.

## Hedgehog Mushroom Pancakes with Chive Butter

Pancakes are an ideal base for subtly flavored wild mushrooms. Pale varieties, in particular the peppery hedgehog fungus, work best and should be softened in butter before they are added to the batter.

### MAKES 12 PANCAKES

*4 tbsp unsalted butter*

*9 oz / 3¼ cups hedgehog fungus, trimmed and chopped*

*2 oz hedgehog fungus, sliced*

#### For the Pancakes

*1½ cups self-rising flour*

*salt and white pepper*

*2 eggs*

*⅞ cup milk*

#### For the Chive Butter

*scant 1 cup fresh finely chopped chives*

*½ cup unsalted butter, softened*

*1 tsp lemon juice*

*1* First make the chive butter. Stir the chopped chives and lemon juice into the butter. Turn out onto a 10 in square of wax paper and form into a sausage. Roll up, twist both ends of the paper and chill in the fridge for about an hour until it is firm.

*2* Melt half of the butter in a large pan, add the chopped mushrooms and sauté over a moderate heat, allowing the mushrooms to soften and the moisture to evaporate. Spread onto a tray and cool. Cook the sliced mushrooms in a pat of butter and set aside.

*3* To make the batter, sift the flour and salt and pepper into a bowl. Beat the eggs into the milk and add to the flour, stirring to make a thick batter. Add the chopped mushrooms.

*4* Heat the remaining butter in the pan, arrange five slices of mushrooms at a time in the bottom, then spoon the batter into 2 in circles over each mushroom. When bubbles appear on the surface, turn the pancakes over and cook for another 10–15 seconds. Serve warm with slices of chive butter.

## Miso Shiitake Breakfast Soup

This Japanese breakfast soup provides a light nourishing start to the day. It is flavored with shiitake mushrooms and a soy protein called miso. Both are available from health food stores.

### SERVES 4

| |
| --- |
| *3 shiitake mushrooms, fresh or dried* |
| *5 cups water, boiling* |
| *3 tbsp light miso paste* |
| *4 oz bean curd (tofu), cut into large dice* |
| *1 scallion, green part only, sliced* |

*1* If using dried mushrooms, soak in warm water for 20 minutes then drain. Slice the mushrooms thinly. Pour the boiling water into a saucepan. Stir in the miso, add the mushrooms and simmer for 5 minutes.

*2* Divide the bean curd among four warmed soup bowls, ladle in the broth, scatter with sliced scallion and serve.

### Cook's Tip
Miso is a fermented soybean paste that varies in strength and color according to the maturity of the soybeans.

## Home-baked Chanterelle Croissant

Chanterelle mushrooms will make a delicious filling and can be added to quick-bake croissants for an unusual and satisfying breakfast. The filling can be made well in advance and goes a long way.

### SERVES 4

| |
| --- |
| *2 tbsp unsalted butter* |
| *4 oz / 1¼ cups fresh chanterelle mushrooms, trimmed and sliced, or ½ oz / ¼ cup dried, soaked in warm water, drained and sliced* |
| *4 tbsp heavy cream* |
| *1 tbsp medium sherry or Madeira* |
| *salt and freshly ground black pepper* |
| *1 package quick-bake croissants* |
| *1 egg, beaten* |

*1* Preheat the oven as directed on the package for the croissants. Melt the butter in a saucepan, add the chanterelles and sauté gently for 3–4 minutes to soften without letting them color. Add the cream and sherry, increase the heat and allow the moisture to evaporate. Season to taste and cool.

*2* Lay the croissant dough shapes out on a floured surface. Place a spoonful of the mixture at the wide end of each triangle. Brush the pointed end of each triangle with beaten egg and roll up, enclosing the filling.

*3* Arrange the croissants on a baking sheet, brush with a little more beaten egg and bake in the oven according to instructions on the package. Serve warm.

### Cook's Tip
Other firm mushrooms can be used as a filling for the croissants. They might include ceps, bay bolete, winter chanterelles, morel, saffron milk caps, hedgehog fungus, field and horse mushrooms, oyster and matsukake mushrooms.

## Mushrooms in a Tarragon Cream Sauce

When your search for wild mushrooms yields only a few specimens and you have to provide breakfast for the proverbial five thousand, combine what you have with a few cultivated mushrooms – enhanced here in a creamy tarragon sauce.

### SERVES 4

| |
| --- |
| 4 tbsp unsalted butter, plus extra for spreading |
| 2 shallots, finely chopped |
| 2–8 oz / ½–3 cups wild mushrooms such as hen of the woods, honey mushrooms, chanterelles, winter chanterelles, ceps, chicken of the woods, parasol mushrooms or hedgehog fungus, trimmed and sliced |
| 12 oz / 3½ cups Cremini mushrooms, trimmed and sliced |
| ⅔ cup heavy cream |
| 3 tbsp chopped fresh tarragon |
| 4 slices brown or white bread |

*1* Melt the butter in a large nonstick frying pan, add the shallots and sauté over a gentle heat until they are soft, without letting them color.

**Cook's Tip**
Almost any variety of mushrooms can be used in a cream sauce, but do avoid dark specimens which can turn the sauce gray.

*2* Add your chosen mushrooms and cook over a moderate heat to soften. Add the cream and tarragon, increase the heat and cook until thick and creamy.

*3* Toast the bread and spread with butter. Spoon over the mushroom mixture and serve at once.

## Saffron Milk-caps with Parsley, Butter and Pine Nuts

Serving wild mushrooms on toast is a quick, easy way to appreciate their individual flavors. Butter-fried saffron milk caps are good, served with a handful of chopped parsley and a sprinkling of toasted pine nuts.

### SERVES 4

| |
| --- |
| ¼ cup pine nuts |
| 1 tsp vegetable oil |
| 4 tbsp unsalted butter, plus extra for spreading |
| 1 shallot, finely chopped |
| 12 oz / 3½ cups saffron milk-caps, trimmed and sliced |
| 3 tbsp heavy cream |
| 5 tbsp chopped fresh parsley |
| salt and freshly ground black pepper |
| 4 slices brown or white bread |

*1* Sauté the pine nuts in the oil, tilting the pan, and brown over a moderate heat. Set aside.

*2* Soften the shallot in half the butter. Add the mushrooms and remaining butter and cook until soft. Stir in the cream and cook until thick. Stir in the parsley and season to taste.

*3* Toast the bread and spread with butter. Spoon the mushroom mixture over the toast, sprinkle with toasted pine nuts and serve.

**Cook's Tip**
Saffron milk caps have hollow stems which can harbor insect larvae. Be sure to avoid any that are infested.

## Bacon, Egg and Chanterelle Sandwiches

When mid-morning hunger strikes, few mushroom hunters can resist a plate of egg and bacon sandwiches stuffed with chanterelles.

### SERVES 4

| |
|---|
| 12 oz bacon |
| 4 tbsp unsalted butter, plus extra for spreading |
| 4 oz / 1¼ cups chanterelle mushrooms, trimmed and halved |
| 4 tbsp peanut oil |
| 4 eggs |
| 4 large whole grain rolls, split |
| salt and freshly ground black pepper |

*1* Place the bacon in a large nonstick frying pan and sauté in its own fat until crisp. Transfer to a plate, cover and keep warm.

**Cook's Tip**

For best effect, let the aroma of frying bacon and mushrooms fill the breakfast room.

*2* Melt 2 tbsp of the butter in the pan, add the chanterelles and sauté gently until soft without letting them color. Transfer to a plate, cover and keep warm.

*3* Melt the remaining butter, add the oil and heat to a moderate temperature. Break the eggs into the pan and fry as you like them, sunny side up or over easy.

*4* Toast the rolls, spread with butter, then layer with bacon, chanterelles and a fried egg. Season, top with the second half of the roll and serve.

# Chicken of the Woods Cornbread with Bacon and Tomatoes

Savory cornbread is a welcome sight at breakfast time and is really delicious with crispy broiled bacon and tomatoes.

### SERVES 4

| |
| --- |
| 2 tbsp butter |
| 2 oz / ¾ cup chicken of the woods, trimmed and finely chopped |
| 1 cup all-purpose flour |
| ¾ cup fine cornmeal |
| 2 tsp baking powder |
| ½ tsp salt |
| ½ tsp sugar |
| ⅔ cup milk |
| 2 eggs |
| 3 oz corn, canned or frozen |
| 12 oz bacon |
| 4 tomatoes, halved |
| salt and freshly ground black pepper |
| 1 bunch watercress, to garnish |

**Cook's Tip**
For individual shapes, spoon the cornbread mixture into greased muffin tins and bake for 10–12 minutes at 425°F.

1 Preheat oven to 400°F. Melt the butter in a frying pan, add the chicken of the woods and sauté over a low heat for 5 minutes, then set aside to cool. Lightly oil a 3¾ cup loaf pan then line with wax paper.

2 Sift the flour, cornmeal, baking powder, salt and sugar into a bowl. Add the milk, eggs, corn and mushrooms. Stir to make batter.

3 Preheat the broiler to a moderate temperature. Meanwhile, turn the batter into the prepared pan and bake near the top of the oven for 25 minutes. Allow to cool slightly.

4 Arrange the bacon and tomato halves on a tray or broiler pan and season the tomatoes with salt and pepper. Broil until the bacon is golden, turning once.

5 Lift the cornbread out of the pan and cut into thick slices. Serve with the broiled bacon and tomatoes, garnished with watercress.

## Champagne Truffle Breakfast

When you have something to cele-brate, start the day with a stylish breakfast. Scrambled eggs with fresh truffles are a treat with toasted brioche and Champagne. For the best flavor, it is worth tracking down fresh black and white truffles. Pre-served truffles offer little if any flavor and benefit from a drop or two of truffle oil.

| SERVES 4 |
| --- |
| 4 brioches |
| 8 fresh farm eggs |
| 4 tbsp crème fraîche |
| 3 drops truffle oil (optional) |
| salt and freshly ground black pepper |
| 1 fresh black truffle |
| 2 tbsp unsalted butter, plus extra for spreading |
| Champagne, to serve |

*1* Preheat a moderate broiler. Slice the brioche, toast and keep warm.

*4* Butter the toasted brioches and arrange on four plates.

*2* Break the eggs into a bowl, add the crème fraîche and truffle oil, if using, season and beat with a fork. Then slice half of the truffle finely into the egg mixture.

*5* Spoon the scrambled egg onto each slice of brioche and scatter with truffle shavings. Serve with Champagne.

*3* Melt the butter in the frying pan, pour in the eggs and with a flat wooden spoon stir around the base of the pan until lightly scrambled.

**Cook's Tip**
To ensure scrambled eggs are soft and creamy, they should be taken off the heat while a little underdone.

**Cook's Tip**
When using truffle oil, never be tempted to add more than a few drops. If too much of this precious oil is used its flavor will become bitter to taste.

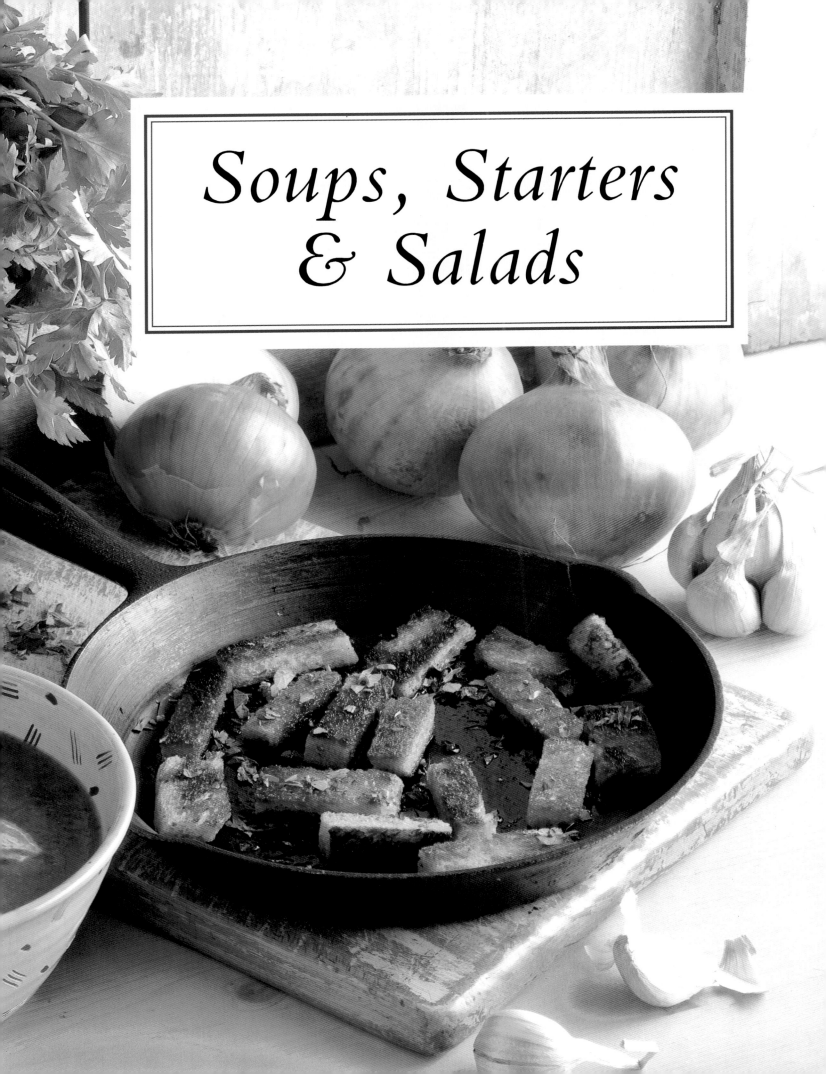

# Soups, Starters
# & Salads

# Buckwheat Blinis with Mushroom Caviar

These little Russian pancakes are traditionally served with fish roe caviar and soured cream. The term caviar is also given to fine vegetable mixtures called ikry. This wild mushroom ikry caviar is popular in the autumn and has a silky rich texture.

### SERVES 4

| |
|---|
| 1 cup all-purpose flour |
| 1/3 cup buckwheat flour |
| 1/2 tsp salt |
| 1 1/4 cups milk |
| 1 tsp dry yeast |
| 2 eggs, separated |

### For the Caviar

| |
|---|
| 12 oz / 3 1/2 cups mixed assorted wild mushrooms such as field mushrooms, queen bolete, bay boletes, oyster and honey mushrooms |
| 1 tsp celery salt |
| 2 tbsp walnut oil |
| 1 tbsp lemon juice |
| 3 tbsp chopped fresh parsley |
| freshly ground black pepper |
| scant 1 cup sour cream or crème fraîche |

*1* To make the caviar, trim and chop the mushrooms, then place them in a glass bowl, toss with the celery salt and cover with a weighted plate.

*2* Let the mushrooms stand for 2 hours until the juices have run out into the bottom of the bowl. Rinse the mushrooms thoroughly to remove the salt, drain and press out as much liquid as you can with the back of a spoon. Return them to the bowl and toss with walnut oil, lemon juice, parsley and a twist of pepper. Chill.

*3* Sift the two flours together with the salt in a large mixing bowl. Heat the milk to approximately body temperature. Add the yeast, stirring until dissolved, then pour into the flour, add the egg yolks and stir to make a smooth batter. Cover with a damp cloth and leave in a warm place.

*4* Whisk the egg whites in a clean bowl until stiff, then fold into the risen batter.

*5* Heat a cast-iron pan or griddle to a moderate temperature. Moisten with oil, then drop spoonfuls of the batter onto the surface. When bubbles rise to the surface, turn them over and cook briefly on the other side. Spoon on the sour cream, top with the mushroom caviar and serve.

## Wild Mushroom Tapenade Toasts

Tapenade is a paste made from black olives, garlic, anchovies, capers, olive oil and lemon. A little goes a long way. Here it is spread on bread, toasted and topped with wild mushrooms and hard-boiled eggs.

### SERVES 4

*12 oz / 3½ cups strongly flavored wild mushrooms such as ceps, bay boletes, chicken of the woods, saffron milk-caps and chanterelles, trimmed and sliced*

*4 tbsp unsalted butter*

*½ lemon*

*salt and freshly ground black pepper*

*4 small eggs*

*1 French loaf, sliced*

*1 small bunch parsley, to garnish*

### For the Tapenade

*5 oz / 1 cup Kalamata olives, pitted*

*1 garlic clove, peeled*

*5 anchovy fillets*

*1 tbsp capers*

*2 tbsp olive oil*

*juice of ½ lemon*

### Cook's Tip

If you don't have time to make your own tapenade, buy it ready-made from delicatessens and specialist food stores.

*1* Sauté the mushrooms gently in butter for 6–8 minutes to soften, then increase heat to evaporate the juices. Add a generous squeeze of lemon and season to taste. Transfer to a bowl, cover and keep warm.

*2* To make the tapenade, place all the tapenade ingredients in a food processor and blend to a fine paste. Boil the eggs for 10 minutes.

*3* Preheat a broiler to a moderate temperature. Meanwhile cool the eggs under running cold water, peel and cut into quarters. Then slice the French loaf diagonally and toast on one side. Spread the other side thinly with tapenade and toast again.

*4* Heap each piece of toast with wild mushrooms, top with a section of hard-boiled egg and garnish with a sprig of parsley.

## French Onion and Morel Soup

French onion soup is appreciated for its light beefy taste. Few improvements can be made to this classic soup, but a few richly scented morel mushrooms will impart a worthwhile flavor.

### SERVES 4

| |
|---|
| 4 tbsp unsalted butter, plus extra for spreading |
| 1 tbsp vegetable oil |
| 3 medium onions, sliced |
| 3¾ cups beef stock |
| 5 tbsp Madeira or sherry |
| 8 medium dried morel mushrooms |
| 4 slices French bread |
| 1 cup Gruyère, Beaufort or Fontina cheese, grated |
| 2 tbsp chopped fresh parsley |

1 Melt the butter and oil in a large frying pan, add the onions and cook for 10–15 minutes until the onions are a rich mahogany brown color.

### Cook's Tip
The flavor and richness of this soup will improve with keeping. Refrigerate for up to 5 days.

2 Transfer the browned onions to a large saucepan, cover with beef stock, add the Madeira and the morels, then simmer for 20 minutes.

3 Preheat the broiler to a moderate temperature and toast the French bread on both sides. Spread one side with butter and heap with grated cheese. Ladle the soup into four flameproof bowls, float the cheese toasts on top and broil until crisp and brown. Alternatively, broil the cheese-topped toast, place one slice in each warmed soup bowl and ladle the hot soup over. The toast will float to the surface. Sprinkle with chopped parsley and serve.

## Cep Soup with Parsley Croutons

The lasting aroma of the cep mushroom is caught in this delicious soup.

### SERVES 4

| |
|---|
| 4 tbsp unsalted butter |
| 2 medium onions, finely chopped |
| 1 garlic clove |
| 8 oz / 2½ cups fresh ceps or bay bolete, sliced, or 1 oz / ½ cup dried |
| 5 tbsp dry white wine |
| 3¾ cups chicken stock, boiling |
| 4 oz floury potatoes, peeled and diced |
| 1 sprig thyme |
| 1 tbsp lemon juice |
| salt and freshly ground black pepper |

### For the Croutons

| |
|---|
| 3 slices day-old bread |
| 4 tbsp butter |
| 3 tbsp finely chopped fresh parsley |

1 Melt the butter in a large saucepan, add the onions and brown lightly. Add the garlic, ceps and wine. Add the stock, potatoes and thyme. Simmer gently for 45 minutes.

2 Purée the soup in just a few short bursts so that pieces of mushroom are left intact. Season with lemon juice and salt and pepper.

### Cook's Tip
A variation on this soup can be made with the same quantity of dried saffron milk caps or half the quantity of dried morel mushrooms.

3 To make the croutons, cut the bread into 1 in fingers. Melt the butter in a large frying pan, toss in the fingers of bread and fry until golden. Add the parsley and combine. Ladle the soup into warmed soup bowls, sprinkle with parsley croutons and serve.

## Tortellini Chanterelle Broth

The savory-sweet quality of chanterelle mushrooms combines well in a simple broth with spinach-and-ricotta-filled tortellini. Serve as a starter or light main course.

### SERVES 4

| |
|---|
| *12 oz fresh spinach and ricotta tortellini, or 6 oz dried* |
| *5 cups chicken broth* |
| *5 tbsp dry sherry* |
| *6 oz / 1¾ cups fresh chanterelle mushrooms, trimmed and sliced, or ½ oz / ¼ cup dried* |
| *chopped fresh parsley, to garnish* |

*1* Cook the tortellini according to the package instructions.

*2* Bring the chicken broth to a boil, add the sherry and mushrooms and simmer for 10 minutes.

*3* Strain the tortellini, add to the stock, ladle into four warmed soup bowls and garnish with the chopped parsley.

### Cook's Tip
For a lighter version, replace the tortellini with 2 cups dried vermicelli pasta.

## Champignons de Paris à la Grècque

Cultivated mushrooms are often criticized by serious mushroom pickers for a lack of flavor, but the *champignon de Paris* or Cremini mushroom is an improvement on the ubiquitous button mushroom.

### SERVES 4

| |
|---|
| *3 tbsp olive oil* |
| *15 little white onions, peeled* |
| *½ garlic clove, crushed* |
| *1½ lb / 6 cups Cremini mushrooms or closed field mushrooms, halved or quartered if large* |
| *1¼ cups homemade or canned chicken broth, boiling* |
| *5 tbsp white wine* |
| *2 tsp black peppercorns* |
| *4 tsp coriander seeds* |
| *1 sprig thyme* |
| *1 small bay leaf* |
| *salt and freshly ground black pepper, if necessary* |
| *1 tbsp wine vinegar* |
| *15 cherry tomatoes* |

*1* Heat the olive oil in a large nonstick frying pan. Add the onions and brown gently over a low heat. Add the garlic and the mushrooms, stir and sauté gently until the mushrooms soften and the juices begin to run. Transfer to a large saucepan.

### Cook's Tip
The flavor of these mushrooms will improve if kept refrigerated for up to a week. To peel little white onions, cover with boiling water to soften their skins.

*2* Add the stock, wine, peppercorns, coriander seeds, thyme and bay leaf. Cover the surface with a round of wax paper. Simmer for 15 minutes. Add the vinegar and season if required.

*3* Cover the cherry tomatoes with boiling water to loosen their skins, peel and add to the onion and mushroom mixture. Allow to cool to room temperature and serve with a basket of coarse textured bread.

## Salad of Fresh Ceps with a Parsley, Egg and Walnut Dressing

To capture the just picked flavor of a cep or bay bolete, consider this delicious salad enriched with an egg yolk and walnut oil dressing. Choose small ceps and bay boletes for a firm texture and a fine flavor.

### SERVES 4

| |
| --- |
| 12 oz / 3½ cups fresh ceps or bay boletes |
| 6 oz mixed salad leaves, to include: escarole, young spinach and frisée |
| salt and freshly ground black pepper |
| ½ cup small walnut pieces, toasted |
| 2 oz fresh Parmesan cheese |

### For the Dressing

| |
| --- |
| 2 egg yolks |
| ½ tsp French mustard |
| 5 tbsp peanut oil |
| 3 tbsp walnut oil |
| 2 tbsp lemon juice |
| 2 tbsp chopped fresh parsley |
| 1 pinch superfine sugar |

**Cook's Tip**

For special occasions, 2–3 drops of truffle oil will impart a deep and mysterious flavor of the forests.

*1* Place the egg yolks in a screw top jar with the mustard, peanut and walnut oil, lemon juice, parsley and sugar. Shake well.

*2* Slice the mushrooms thinly.

*3* Place the mushrooms in a large salad bowl and combine with the dressing. Leave for 10–15 minutes for the flavors to mingle.

*4* Wash and dry the salad leaves, then toss with the mushrooms.

*5* Turn out onto four large plates, season well, then scatter with toasted walnuts and shavings of Parmesan cheese.

**Cook's Tip**

Be sure to use only the freshest eggs from a reputable supplier. Expectant mothers, young children and the elderly are advised not to eat raw egg yolks. If this presents a problem, the dressing can be made without the egg yolks, or with yolks cooked for 3–4 minutes.

## Stuffed Garlic Mushrooms with Prosciutto and Herbs

**SERVES 4**

| 1 medium onion, chopped |
| --- |
| 6 tbsp unsalted butter |
| 8 medium field mushrooms |
| ½ oz / ¼ cup dried ceps, bay boletes or saffron milk-caps, soaked in warm water for 20 minutes |
| 1 garlic clove, crushed |
| ¾ cup fresh bread crumbs |
| 1 egg |
| 5 tbsp chopped fresh parsley |
| 1 tbsp chopped fresh thyme |
| salt and freshly ground black pepper |
| 4 oz prosciutto di Parma or San Daniele, thinly sliced |
| fresh parsley, to garnish |

**Cook's Tip**
Garlic mushrooms can be easily prepared in advance ready to go into the oven.

*1* Preheat the oven to 375 °F. Sauté the onion gently in half the butter for 6–8 minutes until soft but not colored. Meanwhile, break off the stems of the field mushrooms, setting the caps aside. Drain the dried mushrooms and chop these and the stems of the field mushrooms finely. Add to the onion together with the garlic and cook for another 2–3 minutes.

*2* Transfer the mixture to a bowl, add the bread crumbs, egg, herbs and seasoning. Melt the remaining butter in a small pan and generously brush over the mushroom caps. Arrange the mushrooms on a baking sheet and spoon in the filling. Bake in the oven for 20–25 minutes until well browned.

*3* Top each with a strip of prosciutto, garnish with parsley and serve.

## Mushroom Salad with Parma Ham

**SERVES 4**

| 3 tbsp unsalted butter |
| --- |
| 1 lb / 4½ cups assorted wild and cultivated mushrooms such as chanterelles, ceps, bay boletes, honey mushrooms, oyster, field and Cremini mushrooms, trimmed and sliced |
| 4 tbsp Madeira or sherry |
| juice of ½ lemon |
| ½ head of oak leaf lettuce |
| ½ head of frisée lettuce |
| 2 tbsp walnut oil |
| **For the Pancake Ribbons** |
| 3 tbsp all-purpose flour |
| 5 tbsp milk |
| 1 egg |
| 4 tbsp freshly grated Parmesan cheese |
| 4 tbsp chopped fresh herbs such as parsley, thyme, marjoram or chives |
| salt and freshly ground black pepper |
| 6 oz Parma ham, thickly sliced |

*1* To make the pancakes, blend the flour and the milk. Beat in the egg, cheese, herbs and seasoning. Pour enough of the mixture into a frying pan to coat the bottom. When the batter has set, turn the pancake over and cook briefly on the other side.

*3* Gently sauté the mushrooms in the remaining butter for 6–8 minutes until the moisture has evaporated. Add the Madeira and lemon juice, and season to taste.

*2* Turn out and cool. Roll up the pancake and slice thinly to make ½ in ribbons. Cook and cut the remaining batter in the same way and cut the ham into similar sized ribbons. Toss with the pancake ribbons.

*4* Toss the salad leaves in the oil and arrange on four plates. Place the ham and pancake ribbons in the center, spoon on the mushrooms and serve.

## Woodland Salsa Dip

This is good with mushrooms that become very soft in cooking. Firmer-fleshed mushrooms can be added to provide texture and flavor.

### SERVES 4

| |
|---|
| 5 tbsp olive oil |
| 1 medium onion, chopped |
| 1 garlic clove, crushed |
| 1 lb eggplant, chopped |
| 12 oz / 3½ cups shaggy ink caps, puffballs and slippery jacks, trimmed and chopped |
| 3 oz / 1 cup chanterelles, charcoal burners, or saffron milk-caps, trimmed and chopped |
| 3 tbsp chopped fresh parsley, chervil and chives |
| 1 tbsp balsamic vinegar |
| salt and freshly ground black pepper |

### For Dipping

| |
|---|
| sesame bread sticks, celery, carrot, baby corn, strips of toasted pita bread |

*1* Heat 1 tbsp of the olive oil in a heavy saucepan over a moderate heat, add the onion and cook gently to soften without coloring.

*2* Stir in the remaining oil, the garlic and eggplant, then cover and cook for 10 minutes. Add the mushrooms and cook uncovered for a further 15 minutes.

*3* Stir in the herbs and vinegar and season to taste. Allow to cool and serve with bread sticks, pita bread and raw vegetables.

### Cook's Tip

Woodland salsa dip will keep in the fridge in a covered container for 10 days. Do not freeze it.

---

## Spinach and Wild Mushroom Soup

### SERVES 4

| |
|---|
| 2 tbsp unsalted butter |
| 1 medium onion, chopped |
| 12 oz / 3½ cups assorted wild and cultivated mushrooms such as ceps, bay boletes, queen bolete, shaggy ink caps, field, oyster and shiitake mushrooms, trimmed and chopped |
| 1 garlic clove, crushed |
| 2 tsp chopped fresh thyme or dill or 1 tsp dried |
| 5 cups boiling homemade or canned chicken or vegetable broth |
| 3 oz floury potato, finely chopped |
| 14 oz fresh spinach, trimmed, or 7 oz frozen chopped spinach, defrosted and drained |
| salt and freshly ground black pepper |
| pinch of grated nutmeg |
| 4 tbsp heavy or sour cream, to serve |

### Cook's Tip

If fresh wild mushrooms are unavailable, use 8 oz / 2½ cups cultivated field mushrooms with ½ oz / ¼ cup dried ceps, bay boletes or saffron milk caps.

*1* Melt the butter in a large pan, add the onion and sauté gently without coloring for 6–8 minutes. Add the mushrooms, garlic and herbs, cover and allow the juices to run.

*2* Add half of the broth, the potato and spinach. Bring back to a boil and simmer for 10 minutes.

*3* Purée the soup and return to the saucepan. Add the remaining stock and season to taste with salt, pepper and a little nutmeg. Serve with a dollop of cream stirred into the soup.

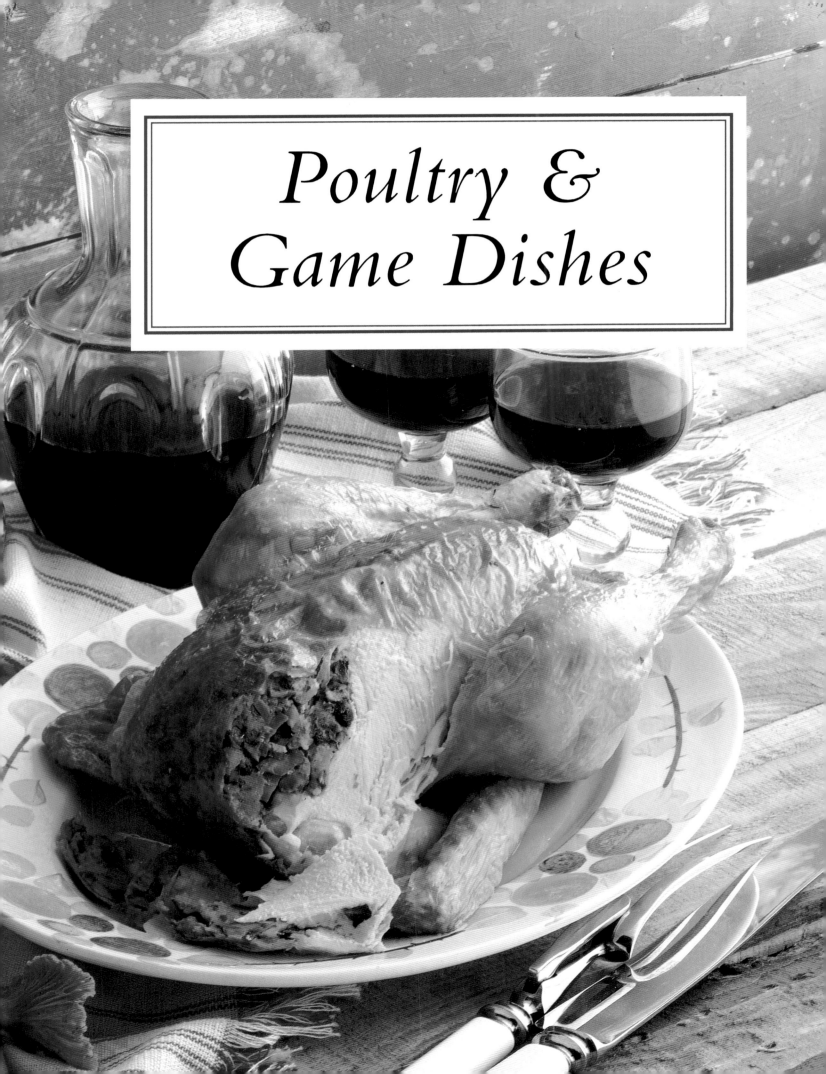

# Poultry &
# Game Dishes

## Mushroom Picker's Chicken Paella

A good paella is based on a few well chosen ingredients. Here, wild mushrooms combine with chicken and vegetables.

### SERVES 4

| |
| --- |
| *3 tbsp olive oil* |
| *1 medium onion, chopped* |
| *1 small bulb fennel, sliced* |
| *8 oz / 2½ cups assorted wild and cultivated mushrooms such as ceps, bay boletes, chanterelles, saffron milk-caps, hedgehog fungus, matsutake, honey and oyster mushrooms, trimmed and sliced* |
| *1 garlic clove, crushed* |
| *3 free range chicken legs, chopped through the bone* |
| *1²/3 cups short-grain Spanish or Italian rice* |
| *3¾ cups homemade or canned chicken broth, boiling* |
| *1 pinch saffron strands or 1 individual tube of saffron powder* |
| *1 sprig thyme* |
| *14 oz can wax beans, drained* |
| *¾ cup frozen peas* |

### Cook's Tip

For a vegetarian mushroom paella, omit the chicken, replace the chicken broth with vegetable broth and if you can, include chicken of the woods in your choice of mushrooms.

*1* Heat the olive oil in a 14 in paella pan or a large frying pan. Add the onion and fennel and sauté over a low heat for 3–4 minutes.

*3* Stir in the rice, add the broth, saffron, thyme, wax beans and peas. Bring to a simmer and then cook gently for 15 minutes without stirring.

*2* Add the mushrooms and garlic, and cook until the juices begin to run, then increase the heat to evaporate the juices. Push the onion and mushrooms to one side. Add the chicken pieces and sauté briefly.

*4* Remove from the heat and cover the surface of the paella with a circle of greased wax paper. Cover the paper with a clean dish towel and allow the paella to finish cooking in its own heat for about 5 minutes. Bring to the table, uncover and serve.

# "Chicken" of the Woods Polenta with a Cauliflower Fungus Cream

This dish contains no chicken at all and will please both meat eaters and vegetarians alike. So convincing is the flavor and texture of chicken of the woods, that many people will find it difficult to believe that they're not actually eating chicken.

### SERVES 4

| |
|---|
| 1 lb small new potatoes |
| 5½ cups homemade or canned light vegetable stock, boiling |
| 6 oz young carrots, trimmed and peeled |
| 6 oz sugar snap peas |
| 4 tbsp unsalted butter |
| 3 oz / 1 cup honey mushrooms or hedgehog fungus, trimmed and sliced |
| 5 horn of plenty, fresh or dried, chopped |
| 1½ cups quick-cooking fine polenta or cornmeal |
| 2 shallots or 1 small onion, chopped |
| 2 fist-sized pieces cauliflower fungus or ½ oz / ¼ cup dried |
| 4 oz / 1¼ cups chicken of the woods, trimmed and sliced |
| ⅔ cup light cream |
| 3 egg yolks |
| 2 tsp lemon juice |
| celery salt and cayenne pepper |

**Cook's Tip**
If preparing this recipe in advance, make the polenta loaf and mushroom and vegetable sauce, then allow to cool. When ready to serve, reheat the polenta and sauce, then thicken the sauce with egg yolks, season and serve.

*1* Lightly oil a 9 in loaf pan and line with a single sheet of wax paper. Set aside. Cover the potatoes with boiling water, add a pinch of salt and cook for 20 minutes. Bring the vegetable broth to a boil, add the carrots and peas and cook for 3–4 minutes. Remove with a slotted spoon and keep warm.

*2* Add 2 tbsp of the butter and the honey mushrooms or hedgehog fungus and horn of plenty to the broth and simmer for 5 minutes. Pour in the polenta in a steady stream and stir for 2–3 minutes until thickened. Turn the polenta into the prepared pan, cover and set aside to become firm.

*3* To make the sauce, melt the remaining butter, add the shallots or onion and cook gently without coloring. Add the cauliflower fungus cut into thumb-sized pieces, with the chicken of the woods, and cook for 2–3 minutes. Add the cream and the reserved cooked vegetables and simmer to evaporate excess moisture.

*4* Remove from the heat, stir in the egg yolks and allow residual heat to slightly thicken the sauce. The sauce must not boil at this stage. Add the lemon juice, then season with celery salt and a dash of cayenne pepper.

*5* To serve, turn the warm polenta out onto a board, slice with a wet knife and arrange on four serving plates. Spoon the mushroom and vegetable sauce over the polenta and serve with the buttered new potatoes.

## Matsutake Chicken Pot Pie

Matsutake is a kingly mushroom most often found in the West. It provides a mild taste and aroma to this trans-Atlantic pot pie. It is perhaps best mixed with bay boletes, saffron milk-caps, parasol mushroom, oyster or closed field mushrooms.

**SERVES 4**

| |
|---|
| 4 tbsp vegetable oil |
| 1 medium onion, chopped |
| 1 celery stalk, sliced |
| 1 small carrot, peeled and cut into julienne strips |
| 2 small chicken breasts, skin and bone removed |
| 1 lb / 4½ cups matsutake mushrooms and a selection of others mentioned above, trimmed and sliced |
| 6 tbsp all-purpose flour |
| 2¼ cups chicken broth, boiling |
| 2 tsp Dijon mustard |
| 2 tbsp medium sherry |
| 2 tsp wine vinegar |
| salt and freshly ground black pepper |
| **For the Pot pie Topping** |
| 2½ cups self-rising flour |
| pinch of celery salt |
| pinch of cayenne pepper |
| ½ cup cold unsalted butter, diced |
| ½ cup Cheddar cheese, grated |
| ⅔ cup cold water |
| 1 beaten egg, to glaze, optional |

*1* Preheat the oven to 400°F. Heat the oil in a large heavy saucepan, add the onion, celery and carrot and sauté gently without coloring, to soften. Cut the chicken breasts into bite-sized pieces, add to the vegetables and cook briefly. Add the mushrooms, sauté until the juices run, then stir in the flour.

*2* Remove the pan from the heat and stir in the broth gradually so that the flour is completely absorbed. Return the pan to the heat, and simmer gently to thicken, stirring all the time. Add the mustard, sherry, vinegar and seasoning. Cover and keep warm.

**Cook's Tip**
This recipe can easily be made as a pie by replacing the topping with a layer of flaky or unsweetened pie pastry.

*3* To make the topping, sift the flour, celery salt and cayenne pepper into a bowl or a food processor fitted with a metal blade. Add the butter and half of the cheese, then either rub the mixture together with your fingers or process until it resembles large fresh bread crumbs. Add the water and combine without overmixing.

*4* Turn out onto a floured board, form into a round and flatten to about a ½ in thickness. Cut out as many 2 in shapes as you can, using a plain cutter.

*5* Transfer the chicken mixture to a 5 cup deep pie dish, then overlap the pastry shapes around the edge. Brush with beaten egg, scatter with the remaining cheese and bake in the oven for 25–30 minutes until the topping is puffed and golden.

## Main Course Soup of Duck, Beets and Ceps

**SERVES 4**

4 tbsp butter

2 medium onions, halved and sliced

2 duck legs or breasts

5 cups chicken broth

6 oz white cabbage, sliced

1 1/2 lb raw beets, chopped

1/2 oz / 1/4 cup dried ceps or bay boletes

1 sprig thyme·

14 oz can wax beans

2 tbsp wine vinegar

salt and freshly ground black pepper

**For the Garnish**

2/3 cup sour cream

2 tbsp horseradish sauce

4 tbsp chopped fresh parsley

*1* Melt the butter in a heavy saucepan, add the onions and brown lightly. Add the duck, cover with broth, then add the cabbage, beets, ceps, thyme and wax beans. Cover and simmer for 1 1/4 hours.

*2* Skim off as much fat as you can. Remove the pieces of duck, slice into thick pieces and return to the pan. Add the vinegar and season to taste.

*3* Blend the sour cream with the horseradish. Ladle the soup into bowls, and add a dollop of horseradish and some parsley. Serve with rye bread.

## Roly Poly Chicken and Chanterelle Pudding

**SERVES 4**

1 medium onion, chopped

1 celery stalk, sliced

2 tsp chopped fresh thyme

2 tbsp vegetable oil

2 chicken breasts, skinned and boned

4 oz / 1 1/4 cups fresh chanterelles, trimmed and sliced, or 1/2 oz / 1/4 cup dried, soaked in warm water for 20 minutes

4 tbsp all-purpose flour

1 1/4 cups homemade or canned chicken broth, boiling

1 tsp Dijon mustard

2 tsp wine vinegar

salt and freshly ground black pepper

**For the Roly Poly Dough**

3 cups self-rising flour

1/2 tsp salt

2/3 cup chilled unsalted butter, diced

5 tbsp cold water

*1* Sauté the onion, celery and thyme gently in oil without coloring. Cut the chicken into bite-sized pieces, add to the pan with the mushrooms and cook briefly. Stir in the flour, then remove from the heat.

*2* Stir in the chicken broth gradually so that the flour is completely absorbed by the broth. Return to the heat, simmer to thicken, then add the mustard, vinegar and seasoning. Set aside to cool.

*3* To make the dough, sift the flour and salt into a bowl. Add the butter, then rub together with the fingers until it resembles coarse bread crumbs. Add the water all at once and combine without overmixing. Roll out the dough on a floured surface into a rectangle 10 × 12 in. Rinse a piece of cheesecloth, about twice as big as the dough, in a little water. Place the dough on the cheesecloth. Spread the cool chicken filling over the dough and roll up from the short end, using the cheesecloth to help, to make a fat sausage. Enclose in cheesecloth and tie each end with string.

*4* Lower the pudding into a pan of boiling water, cover and simmer for 1 1/2 hours. Lift out, untie, slice and serve.

## Wild Rabbit and Mushroom Stew

The rich flavor of wild rabbit echoes the qualities of wild mushrooms.

**SERVES 4**

| |
|---|
| 3 tbsp olive oil |
| 12 button onions, peeled |
| 1 celery stalk, cut into julienne sticks |
| 1 medium carrot, cut into julienne sticks |
| 2 lb wild rabbit portions, trimmed |
| salt and freshly ground black pepper |
| 2 tbsp all-purpose flour |
| 4 oz Jerusalem artichokes, peeled and chopped |
| 2¼ cups chicken broth, boiling |
| 3 oz / 1 cup fresh horn of plenty, trimmed |
| ½ oz / ¼ cup dried ceps or bay boletes |
| 1 tbsp green olive paste |
| 8 green olives |
| 1 tbsp lemon juice |

*1* Heat the olive oil in a heavy skillet, add the onions, celery and carrots and brown lightly for 6–8 minutes. Push to one side of the pan. Season the rabbit, add to the pan and brown quickly. Stir in the flour, add the Jerusalem artichokes, then remove from the heat.

*3* Add the mushrooms and the olive paste, cover and simmer over a low heat for 1 hour. Add the green olives and lemon juice and adjust the seasoning. Serve with parsley potatoes.

*2* Add the chicken broth gradually so that the flour is absorbed.

**Cook's Tip**
Trim away as many of the small rabbit bones as you can.

## Stuffed Fennel

Vegetable fennel divides into neat boat shapes. In this recipe the shapes are baked with a creamy chicken and oyster mushroom filling and served on a bed of rice.

**SERVES 4**

| |
|---|
| 2 large bulbs fennel |
| 3 eggs |
| 2 tbsp butter |
| 1 medium onion, chopped |
| 2 chicken breasts, skinned and boned |
| 8 oz / 2½ cups oyster mushrooms, trimmed and chopped |
| 4 tbsp all-purpose flour |
| 1¼ cups homemade or canned chicken broth, boiling |
| 1 tsp Dijon mustard |
| 2 tbsp sherry |
| salt and freshly ground black pepper |
| parsley sprigs, to garnish |

*1* Preheat the oven to 375 °F. Trim the base of the fennel and pull each bulb apart into four pieces (save the central part). Boil the fennel in salted water for 3–4 minutes, then drain and leave to cool. Boil the eggs for 10 minutes. Cool, peel and set aside.

*2* Finely chop the central part of the fennel. Sauté the fennel and onion gently in butter for 3–4 minutes.

*3* Cut the chicken into pieces and add to the pan with the mushrooms. Cook over a moderate heat for 6 minutes, stirring frequently. Add the flour and remove from the heat.

*4* Gradually add the chicken broth, making sure the flour is completely absorbed by the broth. Return to the heat and simmer until thickened, stirring all the time. Chop one of the eggs into the chicken mixture, add the mustard, sherry and seasoning to taste.

*5* Arrange the fennel in a baking dish. Spoon the filling into each one, cover with foil and bake for 20–25 minutes. Serve on a bed of rice, garnished with eggs and parsley.

## Sherry Braised Guinea Hen with Saffron Milk-caps

### SERVES 4

| |
|---|
| *2 young guinea hens, trussed* |
| *salt and freshly ground black pepper* |
| *4 tbsp unsalted butter* |
| *5 tbsp dry sherry* |
| *2 medium onions, sliced* |
| *1 small carrot, peeled and chopped* |
| *½ celery stalk, chopped* |
| *8 oz / 2½ cups assorted wild mushrooms such as saffron milk-caps or chanterelles, oyster, honey, parasol and field mushrooms, trimmed and sliced* |
| *1⅞ cup homemade or canned chicken broth, boiling* |
| *1 sprig thyme* |
| *1 bay leaf* |
| *1 tbsp lemon juice* |

*1* Preheat the oven to 375°F. Season the guinea hens with salt and pepper. Melt half of the butter in a flameproof casserole, add the birds and turn until browned all over. Transfer to a shallow dish, heat the residue in the pan, pour in the sherry and bring to a boil, stirring to deglaze the pan. Pour this liquid over the birds and set aside.

### Cook's Tip

If fresh wild mushrooms are unavailable substitute with ½ oz / ¼ cup of dried saffron milk-caps or ceps, with 3 oz / 1 cup cultivated oyster or Cremini mushrooms.

*2* Wipe the casserole clean, then melt the remaining butter. Add the onions, carrots and celery. Place the birds on top, cover and cook in the oven for 40 minutes.

*3* Add the chicken broth, thyme and bay leaf. Tie the mushrooms into a 12 in square of cheesecloth. Place in the casserole, cover and return to the oven for a further 40 minutes.

*4* Transfer the birds to a serving platter, remove the thyme and bay leaf and set the mushrooms in the bag aside. Purée the braising liquid and pour back into the casserole. Add the mushrooms from the cheesecloth to the sauce. Season with salt and pepper and add lemon juice to taste. Heat until simmering and serve over the guinea hens or pour into a serving pitcher.

# Braised Pheasant with Ceps, Chestnuts and Bacon

Pheasant at the end of their season are not suitable for roasting, so consider this delicious casserole enriched with wild mushrooms and chestnuts. Allow two birds for four people.

### SERVES 4

| |
|---|
| *2 mature pheasants* |
| *salt and freshly ground black pepper* |
| *4 tbsp butter* |
| *5 tbsp brandy* |
| *12 pearl onions, peeled* |
| *1 celery stalk, chopped* |
| *2 oz smoked bacon, cut into strips* |
| *3 tbsp all-purpose flour* |
| *2¼ cups homemade or canned chicken broth, boiling* |
| *6 oz peeled chestnuts* |
| *12 oz / 3½ cups fresh ceps or bay boletes, trimmed and sliced, or ½ oz / ¼ cup dried, soaked in warm water for 20 minutes* |
| *1 tbsp lemon juice* |
| *watercress sprigs, to garnish* |

*1* Preheat the oven to 325°F. Season the pheasants with salt and pepper. Melt half of the butter in a large flameproof casserole and brown the pheasants over a moderate heat. Transfer to a shallow dish and pour off the cooking fat. Return the casserole to the heat and brown the residue. Stand back and add the brandy (the sudden flames will die down quickly). Stir to loosen the residue with a flat wooden spoon and then pour the juices over the pheasant and set aside.

*2* Wipe the casserole and melt the remaining butter. Lightly brown the onions, celery and bacon. Stir in the flour. Remove from the heat.

*3* Stir in the broth gradually so that it is completely absorbed by the flour. Add the chestnuts, mushrooms, the pheasants and their juices. Bring back to a gentle simmer, then cover and cook in the oven for 1½ hours.

**Cook's Tip**
Cooking and peeling fresh chestnuts can be hard work, so look out for canned or vacuum-packed varieties.

*4* Transfer the pheasants and vegetables to a serving plate. Bring the sauce back to a boil, add the lemon juice and season to taste. Pour the sauce into a pitcher and garnish the birds.

## Chicken Fricassée Forestier

The term fricassée is used to describe a light stew, usually of chicken that is first sautéed in butter. The accompanying sauce can vary, but here wild mushrooms and bacon provide a rich woodland flavor.

### SERVES 4

| |
|---|
| *3 free range chicken breasts, sliced* |
| *salt and freshly ground black pepper* |
| *4 tbsp unsalted butter* |
| *1 tbsp vegetable oil* |
| *4 oz smoked rindless streaky bacon, cut into pieces* |
| *5 tbsp dry sherry or white wine* |
| *1 medium onion, chopped* |
| *12 oz / 3½ cups assorted wild mushrooms such as chanterelles, ceps, bay boletes, horn of plenty, chicken of the woods, hedgehog fungus, saffron milk-caps, closed field mushrooms and cauliflower fungus, trimmed and sliced* |
| *3 tbsp all-purpose flour* |
| *2¼ cups chicken broth* |
| *2 tsp lemon juice* |
| *4 tbsp chopped fresh parsley* |

*1* Season the chicken with pepper. Heat half of the butter and the oil in a large heavy skillet or flameproof casserole and brown the chicken and bacon pieces. Transfer to a shallow dish and pour off any excess fat.

*2* Return the skillet to the heat and brown the residue. Pour in the sherry or wine and stir with a flat wooden spoon to deglaze the pan. Pour the sherry liquid over the chicken and wipe the skillet clean.

**Cook's Tip**
It is worth spending a little extra on properly reared free range chicken. Not only is it less fatty, but it also has a better flavor and texture.

*3* Sauté the onion in the remaining butter until golden brown. Add the mushrooms and cook, stirring frequently, for 6–8 minutes, until their juices begin to run. Stir in the flour, then remove from the heat. Gradually add the chicken broth and stir well until the flour is completely absorbed.

*4* Add the reserved chicken and bacon with the sherry juices, return to the heat and stir to thicken. Simmer for 10–15 minutes and then add the lemon juice, parsley and seasoning. Serve with plain boiled rice, carrots and baby corn.

## Pan Fried "Chicken" of the Woods with a Sherry Cream Sauce

This dish doesn't use real chicken, the flavor, texture and aroma of *Laetiporus sulphureus* or chicken of the woods is so similar to roast chicken that it can be used in place of the real thing. There's no doubt that both vegetarians and meat eaters will enjoy this dish.

### SERVES 4

| |
| --- |
| *4 tbsp unsalted butter* |
| *2 shallots or 1 small onion, chopped* |
| *1 celery stalk, sliced* |
| *½ medium carrot, peeled and sliced* |
| *12 oz / 3½ cups chicken of the woods, trimmed and sliced* |
| *5 tbsp all-purpose flour* |
| *1⅞ cups homemade or canned chicken or vegetable broth* |
| *5 tbsp sherry* |
| *2 tbsp chopped fresh tarragon* |
| *5 tbsp heavy cream* |
| *2 tbsp lemon juice* |
| *celery salt and cayenne pepper* |

**Cook's Tip**
Instead of serving it over pasta, try this recipe as a delicious pie filling. Cover with puff or unsweetened pie pastry and bake for 45–50 minutes at 375°F.

*1* Melt the butter in a large skillet or flameproof casserole, add the shallots or onion, celery and carrot and sauté gently until soft but without coloring.

*3* Gradually add the broth, stirring well so that the flour is absorbed. Heat gently until simmering, stirring all the time, then add the sherry and tarragon and simmer for 6–8 minutes.

*2* Add the chicken of the woods, let them absorb some of the pan juices, then cook for 3–4 minutes. Stir in the flour and remove from the heat.

*4* Just before serving, stir in the cream and lemon juice and season to taste with celery salt and a dash of cayenne pepper. Serve over tagliatelle or fettuccine pasta.

# Wild Duck Roasted with Morels and Madeira

Wild duck has a rich autumnal flavor that combines well with stronger-tasting mushrooms.

### SERVES 4

| |
|---|
| 2 × 2½ lb mallards, dressed and trussed weight |
| salt and freshly ground black pepper |
| 4 tbsp unsalted butter |
| 5 tbsp Madeira or sherry |
| 1 medium onion, halved and sliced |
| ½ celery stalk, chopped |
| 1 small carrot, chopped |
| 10 large dried morel mushrooms |
| 8 oz / 2½ cups blewits, parasol and field mushrooms, trimmed and sliced |
| 2½ cups homemade or canned chicken broth, boiling |
| 1 sprig thyme |
| 2 tsp wine vinegar |
| parsley sprigs and carrot juliennes, to garnish |
| roast potatoes, to serve |

**Cook's Tip**

Mallard is the most popular wild duck, although widgeon and teal are good substitutes. A widgeon will serve two but allow one teal per person.

*2* Heat the remaining butter in a large flameproof casserole and add the onion, celery and carrot. Place the birds on top and cook in the oven for 40 minutes, reserving the juices.

*3* Tie the mushrooms in an 18 in square piece of cheesecloth. Add the broth, pan liquid, thyme and the cheesecloth bag to the casserole. Cover and return to the oven for 40 minutes.

*4* Transfer the birds to a serving platter, remove and discard the thyme and set the mushrooms aside. Purée the braising liquid and pour back into the casserole. Untie the cheesecloth bag and stir the mushrooms into the sauce. Add the vinegar, season to taste and heat through gently. Garnish the ducks with parsley and carrot. Serve with roast potatoes and the Madeira or sherry sauce.

*1* Preheat the oven to 375°F and season the ducks with salt and pepper. Melt half of the butter in a heavy skillet and brown the birds evenly. Transfer to a shallow dish, heat the residue in the pan, pour in the Madeira or sherry and bring to a boil, stirring, to deglaze the pan. Pour this liquid over the birds and set aside.

## Roast Chicken Stuffed with Forest Mushrooms

A good roast chicken is a feast of flavor and succulence. Spend a little more money on a free range bird and let its flavor mingle with the wild aroma of woodland mushrooms.

### SERVES 4

*2 tbsp unsalted butter, plus extra for basting and to finish gravy*

*1 shallot, chopped*

*4 oz / 1¼ cups wild mushrooms such as chanterelles, ceps, bay boletes, oyster, chicken of the woods, saffron milk-caps, and hedgehog fungus, trimmed and chopped*

*⅔ cup fresh white, wheat, or mixed bread crumbs*

*salt and freshly ground black pepper*

*2 egg yolks*

*4–4½ lb free range chicken*

*½ celery stalk, chopped*

*½ small carrot, chopped*

*3 oz potato, peeled and chopped*

*1 cup homemade or canned chicken broth, plus extra if required*

*2 tsp wine vinegar*

*parsley sprigs, to garnish*

**1** Preheat the oven to 425°F. Melt the butter in a saucepan and gently sauté the shallot without letting it color. Add half of the chopped mushrooms and cook for 2–3 minutes until the moisture appears. Remove from the heat, stir in the bread crumbs, seasoning and egg yolks, to bind the mixture.

**2** Spoon the stuffing into the neck of the chicken, enclose and fasten the skin on the underside with a skewer.

**3** Rub the chicken with some extra butter and season well. Put the celery, carrot, potato and remaining mushrooms in the bottom of a roasting pan. Place the chicken on top of the vegetables, add the chicken broth and roast in the oven for 1¼ hours.

**4** Transfer the chicken to a carving board or warmed serving plate, then purée the vegetables and mushrooms. Pour the mixture back into the pan and heat gently, adjusting the consistency with chicken stock if necessary. Taste and adjust seasoning, then add the vinegar and a pat of butter and stir briskly. Pour the sauce into a serving pitcher and garnish the chicken with sprigs of parsley.

**Cook's Tip**
If fresh mushrooms are not available, replace with ½ oz / ¼ cup of the dried equivalent and soak for 20 minutes before using.

## Roast Turkey Flavored with many kinds of Mushrooms

A roast turkey on the festive table tends to look better than it tastes. One sure way to boost its flavor and succulence is to stuff it with the season's wild mushrooms. The gravy too, can be flavored with all kinds of mushrooms.

### SERVES 6–8

*10 lb fresh turkey, dressed weight*

*butter, for basting*

*watercress, to garnish*

### For the Mushroom Stuffing

*4 tbsp unsalted butter*

*1 medium onion, chopped*

*8 oz / 2½ cups wild mushrooms, such as chanterelle, ceps, bay boletes, chicken of the woods, saffron milk-caps, puffballs and honey mushrooms and hedgehog fungus, trimmed and chopped*

*1½ cups fresh white, wheat, or mixed bread crumbs*

*4 oz pork sausages, skinned*

*1 small fresh truffle, sliced (optional)*

*5 drops truffle oil (optional)*

*salt and freshly ground black pepper*

### For the Gravy

*5 tbsp medium sherry*

*1⅔ cups chicken broth*

*½ oz / ¼ cup dried ceps, soaked*

*4 tsp cornstarch*

*1 tsp Dijon mustard*

*½ tsp wine vinegar*

*salt and freshly ground black pepper*

*1* Preheat the oven to 425°F. To make the stuffing, melt the butter in a saucepan, add the onion and sauté gently without coloring. Add the mushrooms and stir until their juices begin to flow. Remove from the heat, add the bread crumbs, sausage meat and the truffle and truffle oil if using, season and stir well to combine.

*2* Spoon the stuffing into the neck cavity of the turkey and enclose, fastening the skin on the underside with a skewer.

*3* Rub the skin of the turkey with butter, place in a large roasting pan and roast uncovered in the oven for 50 minutes. Lower the temperature to 350°F and cook for another 2 hours and 30 minutes.

*4* To make the gravy, transfer the turkey to a carving board, cover loosely with foil and keep warm. Spoon off the fat from the roasting pan and discard. Heat the remaining liquid until reduced to a solid. Add the sherry and stir briskly with a flat wooden spoon to loosen the residue. Stir in the chicken broth.

*5* Place the cornstarch and mustard in a cup, and blend with 2 tsp water and the wine vinegar. Stir this mixture into the juices in the basting pan and simmer to thicken. Season with salt and pepper and then stir in a pat of butter.

*6* Garnish the turkey with bunches of watercress. Pour the gravy into a serving pitcher and serve separately.

### Cook's Tip
Other sizes of turkey can be cooked this way – allow 1½ lb dressed weight of turkey per person and roast for 20 minutes per 1 lb.

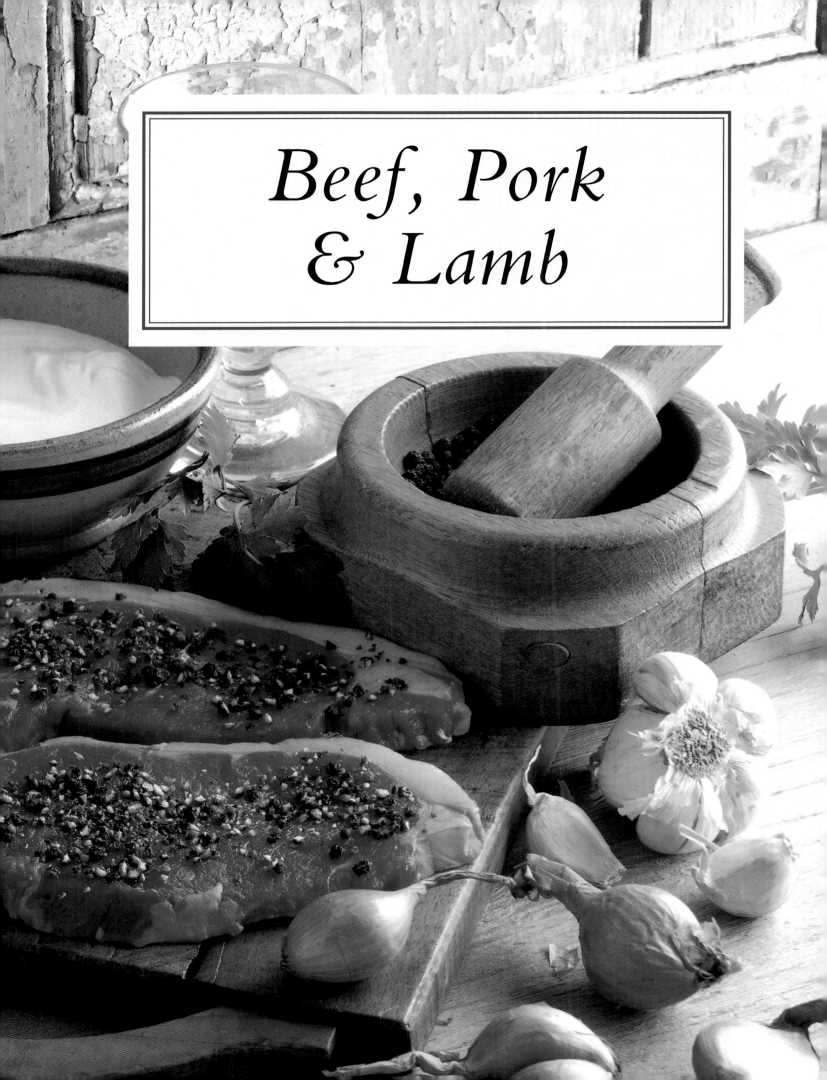

# Beef, Pork
# & Lamb

## Veal Stew with Mushrooms

The combination of ripe tomatoes and tangy orange in this dish brings to mind Mediterranean sunshine. Choose tomatoes grown outside for the very best sundrenched taste.

**SERVES 6**

| |
|---|
| 4 tbsp plain flour |
| 3 lb boneless veal shoulder, cut into 1½ in pieces |
| 2–3 tbsp olive oil |
| 4 or 5 shallots, finely chopped |
| 2 garlic cloves, very finely chopped |
| 1¼ cups dry white wine |
| 1 lb tomatoes, peeled, seeded and chopped |
| grated rind and juice of 1 unwaxed orange |
| bouquet garni |
| 1 tbsp tomato paste |
| 1 tbsp butter |
| ¾ lb button mushrooms, quartered if large |
| salt and freshly ground black pepper |
| chopped fresh parsley, to garnish |

**Cook's Tip**
If shallots are not available, use 1 or 2 mild-flavored red onions instead.

**1** Put the flour in a plastic bag and season with salt and pepper. Drop the pieces of meat into the bag a few at a time and shake to coat with flour, tapping off the excess. Discard the remaining flour.

**2** Heat 2 tbsp of the oil in a flameproof casserole over medium heat. Add enough meat to the pan to fit easily in one layer (do not overcrowd the pan or the meat will not brown). Cook, turning to color all sides, until well browned, then transfer to a plate. Continue browning the meat in batches, adding more oil if needed.

**3** In the same pan, cook the shallots and garlic over medium heat, stirring, until just softened, then stir in the wine and bring to a boil. Return the meat to the pan and add the tomatoes, orange rind and juice, bouquet garni and tomato paste. Bring back to a boil, then reduce the heat to low, cover and simmer gently for approximately 1 hour.

**4** Melt the butter in a frying pan over medium heat and sauté the mushrooms until golden. Add the mushrooms to the casserole and cook, covered, for 20–30 minutes, or until the meat is very tender. Adjust the seasoning and discard the bouquet garni before serving. Garnish the stew with parsley.

## Beef Goulash with Dark Mushrooms and Morels

A good Hungarian goulash is made rich and smooth with onions and paprika. In this recipe dark field mushrooms and morel mushrooms provide extra smoothness and a good depth of flavor.

### SERVES 4

| |
|---|
| 2 lb chuck steak, diced |
| salt and freshly ground black pepper |
| 4 tbsp vegetable oil |
| 2/3 cup red wine |
| 4 medium onions, halved and sliced |
| 1 lb / 4 1/2 cups field or horse mushrooms or closed shaggy ink caps, trimmed and chopped |
| 3 tbsp mild paprika |
| 2 1/2 cups beef broth |
| 2 tbsp tomato paste |
| 1/2 oz / 1/4 cup dried morel mushrooms, soaked in warm water for 20 minutes |
| 1 tbsp wine vinegar |

*1* Preheat the oven to 325°F and season the meat with pepper. Heat half of the oil in a large frying pan and fry the meat over a high heat. A quantity of liquid will appear which must be evaporated before the meat will brown and take on flavor. When the meat has browned, transfer to a flameproof casserole and pour off the fat. Return the frying pan to the heat, add the wine and stir with a flat wooden spoon to deglaze the pan. Pour the liquid over the meat and wipe the pan clean.

*2* Heat the remaining oil in the pan, add the onions and brown lightly.

*3* Add the mushrooms, paprika, broth, tomato paste, the morels and their liquid to the casserole. Bring to a simmer, cover and cook in the oven for about 1 1/2 hours.

### Cook's Tip

Goulash can also be made with diced pork or veal. In this case use chicken broth in place of beef. To keep the goulash a good color, select closed shaggy ink caps that have not started to blacken and deteriorate.

*4* Just before serving, add the vinegar and adjust the seasoning if necessary. Serve with baked potatoes, Savoy cabbage and carrots.

## Cep Meatballs with Roquefort and Walnut Sauce

The salty rich acidity of Roquefort cheese enhances the flavor of good beef. In this recipe meatballs are flavored with cep mushrooms. A Roquefort and walnut sauce makes it a dish to remember.

### SERVES 4

| ½ oz / ¼ cup dried ceps or bay boletes, soaked in warm water for 20 minutes |
| 1 lb lean ground beef |
| 1 small onion, finely chopped |
| 2 egg yolks |
| 1 tbsp chopped fresh thyme |
| celery salt and freshly ground black pepper |
| 2 tbsp olive oil |

### For the Roquefort Sauce

| ⅞ cup milk |
| 2 oz walnuts, toasted |
| 3 slices white bread, crusts removed |
| 3 oz Roquefort cheese |
| 4 tbsp chopped fresh parsley |

*1* Drain the mushrooms, reserving the liquid, and chop finely. Place the beef, onion, egg yolks, thyme and seasoning in a bowl, add the mushrooms and combine well. Divide the mixture into thumb-sized pieces with wet hands and roll into balls.

*2* To make the sauce, place the milk in a small pan and bring to a simmer. Put the walnuts in a food processor and grind until smooth, then add the bread and pour in the milk and reserved mushroom liquid. Add the cheese and parsley, then process until smooth. Transfer to a mixing bowl, cover and keep warm.

*3* Heat the olive oil in a large nonstick frying pan. Cook the meatballs in two batches for 6–8 minutes. Add the sauce to the pan and heat very gently without allowing it to boil, then turn into a serving dish or serve over ribbon pasta.

## Old English Steak and Mushroom Pudding

This pudding has been lost to the fast-food lifestyle. It takes five hours to cook but it is worth waiting for!

### SERVES 4

| 1 lb chuck steak, diced |
| 8 oz / 2½ cups assorted wild and cultivated mushrooms such as chanterelles, ceps, queen bolete, shaggy ink caps, horn of plenty, saffron milk-caps, blewits, oyster, field and honey mushrooms and not more than 3 dried morels, trimmed and sliced |
| 1 medium onion, chopped |
| 3 tbsp all-purpose flour |
| celery salt and freshly ground black pepper |
| 3 shakes Worcestershire sauce |
| ½ cup beef broth |

### For the Pastry Crust

| 2 cups self-rising flour |
| ½ tsp salt |
| 6 tbsp cold butter, grated |
| ⅔ cup cold water |

*1* To make the pastry, sift the flour and salt into a bowl and stir in the butter. Add all of the water and stir with a fork to form a loose dough. Turn out onto a floured surface and press together without overworking.

*2* Brush a 5 cup pudding mold with oil or butter. Roll out the dough with a dusting of flour to form a 10 in circle. Cut out a quarter section and save for the top. Line the mold and set aside.

*3* Mix the beef, mushrooms, onion, flour and seasoning in a large bowl. Transfer to the lined mold, add the Worcestershire sauce and then the beef broth. Bring overlapping pastry edges towards the center, moisten with water and cover the top with the leftover pastry.

*4* Place a circle of wax paper on the pastry, then cover the whole basin with an 18 in piece of foil. Boil 2 in of water in a pan and lower the mold into the pan. Cover and steam for 2½ hours, making sure the water doesn't boil away.

*5* When ready to serve, unmold onto a plate and serve with curly kale, carrots and boiled potatoes.

## Rich Beef Stew with Cep Dumplings

As if the temptation of a rich beef stew isn't enough, here it is crowned with cep dumplings.

**SERVES 4**

| |
|---|
| 4 tbsp vegetable oil |
| 2 lb chuck steak, diced |
| 2/3 cup red wine |
| 2 medium onions, halved and sliced |
| 1/2 celery stalk, chopped |
| lb / 4 1/2 cups open cap wild or cultivated field mushrooms, sliced |
| 1/2 garlic clove, crushed |
| 2 1/2 cups beef broth |
| 2 tbsp tomato paste |
| 2 tsp black olive paste |
| 1 tbsp wine vinegar |
| 1 tsp anchovy sauce |
| 1 sprig thyme |
| salt and freshly ground black pepper |

**For the Cep Dumplings**

| |
|---|
| 2 1/4 cups self-rising flour |
| 1/2 tsp salt |
| 1/2 cup cold butter or margarine, finely diced |
| 3 tbsp chopped fresh parsley |
| 1 tsp chopped fresh thyme |
| 1/2 oz / 1/4 cup dried ceps, soaked in warm water for 20 minutes |
| 1 cup cold milk |

*1* Preheat the oven to 325°F. Lightly season the meat with pepper, then heat half of the oil in a pan, and seal the meat over a high heat. The liquid that appears must be evaporated before the meat will brown.

*2* When the meat has browned, transfer to a flameproof casserole and pour off the fat from the pan. Add the wine to the pan and stir with a flat wooden spoon to loosen the residue. Pour over the meat.

*3* Wipe the pan clean, then heat the remaining oil, add the onions and celery and brown lightly. Add to the casserole with the mushrooms, garlic, beef broth, tomato and olive paste, vinegar, anchovy sauce and thyme. Bring to a simmer, cover and cook in the oven for 1 1/2–2 hours.

*4* To make the dumplings, sift the flour and salt together, add the butter, then the parsley and thyme. Drain the ceps and chop finely. Add the ceps and milk to the mixture and stir with a knife to make a soft dough, taking care not to overmix.

*5* Flour your hands and form the mixture into thumb-sized dumplings. Drop them into simmering water and cook uncovered for 10–12 minutes. When cooked, remove and arrange on top of the stew.

## Braised Beef with Mushroom Gravy

Delicious gravy is an integral part of a good stew.

**SERVES 4**

| |
|---|
| 2 lb chuck steak, sliced |
| salt and freshly ground black pepper |
| 4 tbsp vegetable oil |
| 2/3 cup red wine |
| 2 medium onions, halved and sliced |
| 1/2 celery stalk, chopped |
| 1 lb / 4 1/2 cups open cap wild or cultivated field mushrooms, sliced |
| 1/2 garlic clove, crushed |

| |
|---|
| 2 1/2 cups beef broth |
| 2 tbsp tomato paste |
| 2 tsp black olive paste |
| 1 tsp anchovy sauce |
| 1 sprig thyme |
| 1 tbsp wine vinegar |

*1* Preheat the oven to 325°F. Season the meat with pepper. Heat half of the oil in a large frying pan, and brown the beef over a high heat. Liquid will appear, which must be evaporated before the meat will brown and take on flavor.

*2* Transfer the meat to a flameproof casserole and pour off the fat from the pan. Return the pan to the heat, add the wine and stir briskly. Pour over the meat and wipe the pan clean.

*3* Heat the remaining oil in the pan, add the onions and celery and brown lightly. Add the mushrooms, garlic, beef broth, tomato and olive paste, anchovy sauce and thyme to the casserole. Set over the heat and bring to a simmer. Cover and cook in the oven for about 2 hours until the meat is tender. Add the vinegar and adjust the seasoning. Serve with mashed potatoes, rutabagas and cabbage.

## Lamb Chop Sauté with a Sauce of Woodland Mushrooms

### SERVES 4

| |
|---|
| 4 × 6oz lamb chops |
| salt and freshly ground black pepper |
| 2 tbsp olive oil |
| 1/3 cup red wine |
| 8 oz / 2½ cups assorted wild and cultivated mushrooms, such as chanterelles, ceps, bay boletes, horn of plenty, saffron milk-caps, parasol mushrooms, oyster, puffballs, honey or field mushrooms, trimmed and sliced |
| ½ garlic clove, crushed |
| 7/8 cup homemade or canned chicken broth, boiling |
| 2 tsp cornstarch |
| 1 tsp Dijon mustard |
| ½ tsp black olive paste |
| 1 tsp wine vinegar |
| 2 tbsp unsalted butter |

*1* Season the lamb with black pepper, then moisten with 1 tbsp of the oil. Sauté over a steady heat for 6–8 minutes for medium-rare meat or 12–15 minutes for well done.

### Cook's Tip
Do not season cut pieces of meat with salt before cooking. This can cause the meat to dry and toughen. Season before serving.

*2* Transfer the lamb to a plate, cover and keep warm. Pour off any excess oil from the pan and heat the residue until it browns. Add the red wine and stir with a flat wooden spoon to loosen the residue. Add the mushrooms, stir briefly and then add the chicken broth and simmer for 3–4 minutes.

*3* Place the cornstarch, mustard and olive paste in a cup and blend with 1 tbsp cold water. Stir into the pan and simmer briefly to thicken. Add the vinegar, stir in the butter and season to taste. Season the lamb with a little salt, spoon the sauce over the top and serve with sautéed potatoes, green beans and carrots.

## Black Pepper Beef Steaks with Red Wine and Mushroom Sauce

### SERVES 4

| |
|---|
| 4 × 8oz sirloin or rump steaks |
| 1 tbsp black peppercorns, cracked |
| 1 tbsp olive oil |
| ½ cup red wine |
| 8 oz / 2½ cups assorted wild and cultivated mushrooms such as ceps, bay boletus, chanterelles, horn of plenty, saffron milk-caps, blewits, morels, Paris mushrooms, field, oyster, hen of the woods and honey mushrooms or cauliflower fungus, trimmed and sliced |
| ½ garlic clove, crushed |
| 1¼ cups beef broth |
| 1 tbsp cornstarch |
| 1 tsp Dijon mustard |
| 2 tsp fish sauce (optional) |
| 1 tsp wine vinegar |
| 5 tbsp crème fraîche |

*1* Place a large frying pan over a high heat. Season the steaks with cracked pepper and moisten with oil.

### Cook's Tip
In terms of both flavor and tenderness, the best cut of steak is taken from the rump end. Rib steaks are also good, but because of their size, they are best suited to serve two.

*2* Fry the steaks for 6–8 minutes for medium-rare meat, or 12–15 minutes for well done, turning once. Transfer to a plate and keep warm.

*3* Pour off any excess fat, return the pan to the heat and brown the residue. Add the wine and loosen the residue with a flat wooden spoon. Add the mushrooms and garlic and sauté for 6–8 minutes. Add the stock.

*4* Place the cornstarch and mustard in a cup and blend with 1 tbsp cold water. Stir into the pan juices and simmer to thicken. Add the fish sauce, if using, the vinegar, and the crème fraîche. Spoon the sauce over the steaks and sprinkle with parsley.

## Beef Stroganoff with a Chanterelle Parsley Cream

This dish is believed to be named after a 19th-century Russian diplomat, Count Paul Stroganoff. It was originally made with fillet steak, wild mushrooms and cream, but has suffered many changes. Here is an attempt at the original.

**SERVES 4**

| |
| --- |
| 1 lb fillet or rump steak, trimmed and cut into thin strips |
| salt and freshly ground black pepper |
| 2 tbsp olive oil |
| 3 tbsp brandy |
| 2 shallots, finely chopped |
| 8 oz / 2½ cups chanterelle mushrooms, trimmed and halved |
| ⅔ cup beef stock |
| 5 tbsp sour cream |
| 1 tsp Dijon mustard |
| ½ sweet gherkin, chopped |
| 3 tbsp chopped fresh parsley |

*1* Season the steak with pepper, heat half of the oil in a pan and cook for 2 minutes. Transfer the meat to a plate.

### Cook's Tip
If you can't afford fillet steak, buy best rump or sirloin.

*2* Place the pan over a moderately high heat and brown the sediment. Stand back from the pan, add the brandy, tilt towards the flame (or ignite with a match if cooking on an electric hob) and burn off the liquor vapor. Pour these juices over the meat, cover and keep warm.

*3* Wipe the pan clean, heat the remaining oil and lightly brown the shallots. Add the mushrooms and fry gently for 3–4 minutes to soften.

*4* Add the stock and simmer for a few minutes and then add the sour cream, mustard and gherkin together with the steak and its juices. Simmer briefly, season to taste and stir in the chopped parsley. Serve with buttered noodles dressed with poppy seeds.

## Sauté of Pork with Jerusalem Artichokes and Horn of Plenty

The Jerusalem artichoke has an earthy quality not unlike the flavors of the horn of plenty.

### SERVES 4

| |
|---|
| *3 tbsp vegetable oil* |
| *1 medium onion, halved and sliced* |
| *1 celery stick, sliced* |
| *1 medium carrot, peeled, halved and sliced* |
| *1½ lb lean pork, loin or thick end, cut into strips* |
| *3 tbsp all-purpose flour* |
| *2¼ cups chicken stock* |
| *3 oz Jerusalem artichokes, peeled and thickly sliced* |
| *4 oz / 1¼ cups horn of plenty or winter chanterelles, trimmed* |
| *1 tbsp green olive paste* |
| *1 tbsp lemon juice* |
| *salt and freshly ground black pepper* |

*1* Heat the oil in a heavy skillet or frying pan, add the onion, celery and carrot and fry gently for 6–8 minutes to soften.

*2* Push the vegetables to one side of the pan, add the pork and seal. Stir in the flour and remove from the heat.

*3* Add the stock gradually and stir so that the flour is completely absorbed by the stock.

**Cook's Tip**
Jerusalem artichokes go a long way to provide richness to a dish. If used in excess, however, they sometimes cause flatulence.

*4* Add the artichokes, mushrooms and olive paste and bring to a simmer. Cover with a lid or foil and cook very gently for about 1 hour. Add the lemon juice, adjust the seasoning and serve with a mixture of wild and long grain rice and petits pois.

## Pork Sausage Puff with a Filling of Wild Mushrooms

Fresh pork sausages needn't be cooked in their casing. To make the most of them, remove the meat and wrap it in a puff pastry package. A thick seam of wild mushrooms gives a seasonal twist.

### SERVES 4

| |
|---|
| 4 tbsp unsalted butter |
| ½ garlic clove, crushed |
| 1 tbsp chopped fresh thyme |
| 1 lb / 4½ cups assorted wild and cultivated mushrooms such as ceps, bay boletes, chanterelles, horn of plenty, saffron milk-caps, blewits, chicken of the woods, oyster, field, hen of the woods and honey mushrooms, trimmed and sliced |
| 1 cup fresh white bread crumbs |
| 5 tbsp chopped fresh parsley |
| salt and freshly ground black pepper |
| 12 oz puff pastry, thawed if frozen |
| 1½ lb best pork sausages |
| 1 egg, beaten with a pinch of salt |

*1* Preheat the oven to 350°F. Melt the butter in a large non-stick frying pan, add the garlic, thyme and mushrooms and sauté gently for 5–6 minutes. When the mushroom juices begin to run, increase the heat to evaporate the juices. When dry, stir in the bread crumbs and chopped parsley and season well.

*2* Roll out the pastry on a floured surface to form a 14 × 10 in rectangle and place on a large ungreased baking sheet.

*3* Immerse the sausages in a bowl of water, pierce and pull off their casings. Place half of the sausage meat in a 5 in strip along the center of the pastry. Cover with mushrooms, then with another layer of sausage meat.

*4* Make a series of 1 in slanting cuts in the pastry each side of the filling. Fold the two ends of pastry over the filling, moisten the pastry with beaten egg and then cross the top with alternate strips of pastry from each side. Allow to rest for 40 minutes, brush with a little more egg and bake in the oven for 1 hour.

### Cook's Tip

A good pinch of salt added to a beaten egg will melt down and improve the finished glaze.

## Coriander Lamb Kebabs with Almond Chanterelle Sauce

The delicate sweetness of lamb combines well with apricot-scented chanterelles, used here to make this especially delicious almond sauce.

### SERVES 4

| |
|---|
| 8 lamb cutlets, trimmed |
| 2 tbsp unsalted butter |
| 8 oz / 2½ cups chanterelle mushrooms, trimmed |
| ¼ cup whole almonds, toasted |
| 2 oz white bread, crusts removed |
| 1 cup milk |
| 3 tbsp olive oil |
| ½ tsp superfine sugar |
| 2 tsp lemon juice |
| salt and cayenne pepper |

### For the Marinade

| |
|---|
| 3 tbsp olive oil |
| 1 tbsp lemon juice |
| 2 tsp ground cilantro |
| ½ garlic clove, crushed |
| 2 tsp honey |

*1* Mix all marinade ingredients together, pour over the lamb and leave for at least 30 minutes.

*2* Fry the chanterelles gently in butter without coloring for 3–4 minutes. Set aside.

*3* Place the almonds in a processor and grind finely. Add half of the chanterelles, the bread, milk, oil, sugar and lemon juice, then process.

*4* Preheat a moderate broiler. Thread the lamb onto four metal skewers, and broil for 6–8 minutes on each side. Season the sauce, then spoon over the kebobs. Add the remaining chanterelles and serve with potatoes and a salad.

### Cook's Tip
Almond chanterelle sauce makes a delicious dressing for pasta. Serve with a handful of chanterelles cooked in butter.

## Beef Wellington Enriched with Mushrooms

There are two ways of preparing beef Wellington: both involve a length of beef tenderloin wrapped and baked in flaky pastry. Traditionally the beef is spread with a layer of goose liver pâté, but because of its high price, many cooks turn to an equally delicious and infinitely cheaper pâté of woodland mushrooms.

### SERVES 4

| |
| --- |
| 1½ lb beef tenderloin, tied |
| freshly ground black pepper |
| 1 tbsp vegetable oil |
| 12 oz puff pastry, thawed if frozen |
| 1 egg, beaten, to glaze |
| **For the Parsley Pancakes** |
| 5 tbsp all-purpose flour |
| a pinch of salt |
| ⅔ cup milk |
| 1 egg |
| 2 tbsp chopped fresh parsley |
| **For the Mushroom Pâté** |
| 2 tbsp unsalted butter |
| 2 shallots or 1 small onion, chopped |
| 1 lb / 4½ cups assorted wild and cultivated mushrooms such as oyster mushrooms, ceps, bay boletes, queen bolete, shaggy ink caps, chanterelles, saffron milk caps, parasol mushrooms, blewits, closed field or honey mushrooms, trimmed and chopped |
| 1 cup fresh white bread crumbs |
| 8 tbsp heavy cream |
| 2 egg yolks |

*1* Preheat the oven to 425°F. Season the beef with several twists of black pepper. Heat the oil in a roasting pan, add the beef and quickly sear to brown all sides. Transfer to the oven and roast for 15 minutes for rare, 20 minutes for medium-rare or 25 minutes for well done meat. Set aside to cool. Reduce the temperature to 375°F.

*2* To make the pancakes, beat the flour, salt, half the milk, the egg and parsley together until smooth, then stir in the remaining milk. Heat a greased, nonstick pan and pour in enough batter to coat the bottom. When set, turn over and cook the other side briefly until lightly browned. Continue with remaining batter – the recipe makes three or four.

*3* To make the mushroom pâté, sauté the shallots or onion in butter to soften without coloring. Add the mushrooms and cook until their juices begin to run. Increase the heat and cook briskly so that the juices evaporate. Combine the bread crumbs with the cream and egg yolks. When the mushrooms are dry, add the bread and cream mixture and blend to make a smooth paste. Allow to cool.

### Cook's Tip

Beef Wellington can be prepared up to 8 hours in advance but should be kept at room temperature as the meat will not heat through in the cooking times given if it is chilled before cooking begins. Instead of using a meat thermometer, you can insert a metal skewer into the meat. If the skewer is cold the meat is not done, if it is warm the meat is rare and if it is hot it is well-done.

*4* Roll out the pastry and cut into a rectangle 14 × 12 in. Place two pancakes on the pastry and spread with mushroom pâté. Place the beef on top and spread over any remaining pâté. Cover with the remaining pancakes. Cut out four squares from the corners of the pastry. Moisten the pastry edges with egg and then wrap them over the meat.

*5* Decorate the top with the reserved pastry trimmings, transfer to a baking sheet and rest in a cool place until ready to cook.

*6* Brush evenly with beaten egg. Cook the Wellington for about 40 minutes until golden brown. To ensure that the meat is heated through, test with a meat thermometer. It should read 125–130°F for rare, 135–140°F for medium-rare and 155–160°F for well-done meat.

## Roast Leg of Lamb with a Wild Mushroom Stuffing

When the thigh bone is removed from a leg of lamb, a stuffing can be put in its place. This not only makes the lamb easier to carve but also gives an excellent flavor to the meat.

### SERVES 4

| |
| --- |
| *4 lb leg of lamb, boned* |
| *salt and freshly ground black pepper* |

**For the Wild Mushroom Stuffing**

| |
| --- |
| *2 tbsp butter, plus extra if needed for gravy* |
| *1 shallot or 1 small onion* |
| *8 oz / 2½ cups assorted wild and cultivated mushrooms such as chanterelles, ceps, bay boletes, horn of plenty, blewits, oyster, puffballs, field and honey mushrooms, trimmed and chopped* |
| *½ garlic clove, crushed* |
| *1 sprig thyme, chopped* |
| *1 oz crustless white bread, diced* |
| *2 egg yolks* |
| *salt and freshly ground black pepper* |

**For the Wild Mushroom Gravy**

| |
| --- |
| *3½ tbsp red wine* |
| *1⅔ cups chicken broth, boiling* |
| *⅙ oz / 2 tbsp dried ceps, bay boletes or saffron milk-caps, soaked in boiling water for 20 minutes* |
| *4 tsp cornstarch* |
| *1 tsp Dijon mustard* |
| *½ tsp wine vinegar* |
| *a pat of butter* |
| *watercress, to garnish* |

*1* Preheat the oven to 400°F. To make the stuffing, melt the butter in a large nonstick frying pan and gently fry the shallot or onion without coloring. Add the mushrooms, garlic and thyme and stir until the mushrooms juices begin to run, then increase the heat so that they evaporate completely.

*2* Transfer the mushrooms to a mixing bowl, add the bread, egg yolks and seasoning and mix well. Allow to cool slightly.

*3* Season the inside cavity of the lamb and then press the stuffing into the cavity, using a spoon or your fingers. Tie up the end with fine string and then tie around the lamb so that it does not lose its shape.

*4* Place the lamb in a roasting pan and roast in the oven for 15 minutes per 1 lb for rare meat and 20 minutes per 1 lb for medium-rare. A 4 lb leg will take 1 hour 20 minutes if cooked medium-rare.

*5* Transfer the lamb to a warmed serving plate, cover and keep warm. To make the gravy, spoon off all excess fat from the roasting tin and brown the residue over a moderate heat. Add the wine and stir with a flat wooden spoon to loosen the residue. Add the chicken broth, the mushrooms and their soaking liquid.

*6* Place the cornstarch and mustard in a cup and blend with 1 tbsp water. Stir into the broth and simmer to thicken. Add the vinegar. Season to taste, and stir in the butter. Garnish the lamb with watercress, and serve with roast potatoes, carrots and broccoli.

**Cook's Tip**
If you buy your meat from a butcher, ask for the thigh bone to be taken out.

# Fish &
# Shellfish

## Shellfish Risotto with Fruits of the Forest

The creamy nature of short-grain rice cooked with onions and a simple stock provides the basis for this delicious combination of shellfish and mushrooms.

### SERVES 4

| |
|---|
| *3 tbsp olive oil* |
| *1 medium onion, chopped* |
| *8 oz / 2½ cups assorted wild and cultivated mushrooms such as ceps, bay boletus, chanterelles, chicken of the woods, saffron milk-caps, horn of plenty, wood blewits, oyster, horse mushrooms and truffles, trimmed and sliced* |
| *1 lb / 2¼ cups short-grain Arborio or other short-grained rice* |
| *5 cups homemade or canned chicken or vegetable broth, boiling* |
| *⅔ cup white wine* |
| *4 oz raw shrimp, peeled* |
| *8 oz raw mussels in their shells* |
| *8 oz littleneck clams* |
| *1 medium squid, cleaned, trimmed and sliced* |
| *3 drops truffle oil (optional)* |
| *5 tbsp chopped fresh parsley and chervil* |
| *celery salt and cayenne pepper* |

### Cook's Tip

Before cooking, scrub the mussels and clams, then tap them with a knife. If any of the shells do not close, discard them. After cooking (see step 3), if any of the shells have not opened discard them too.

*1* Heat the oil in a large skillet and sauté the onion for 6–8 minutes until soft but not brown.

*3* Pour in the stock and wine. Add the shrimp, mussels, clams and squid, stir and simmer for 15 minutes.

*2* Add the mushrooms and sauté until their juices begin to run. Stir in the rice and heat through.

*4* Add the truffle oil if using, stir in the herbs, cover and stand for 5–10 minutes. Season to taste with celery salt and a pinch of cayenne pepper and serve with coarse-textured bread.

## Deep Sea Scallops in a Forest of Wild Mushrooms

From the depths of the sea and forest come two flavors that marry perfectly in a smooth creamy sauce.

### SERVES 4

| |
|---|
| 12 oz puff pastry, thawed if frozen |
| 1 egg, beaten, to glaze |
| 6 tbsp unsalted butter |
| 12 scallops, trimmed and thickly sliced |
| salt and freshly ground black pepper |
| 2 shallots, chopped |
| ½ celery stalk, cut into strips |
| ½ medium carrot, peeled and cut into strips |
| 8 oz / 2½ cups assorted wild mushrooms, such as chanterelles, chicken of the woods, cauliflower fungus, oyster, brick caps and honey mushrooms, trimmed and sliced |
| 4 tbsp Noilly Prat or other dry white vermouth |
| ⅔ cup crème fraîche |
| 4 egg yolks |
| 1 tbsp lemon juice |
| celery salt and cayenne pepper |

*1* Roll the pastry out on a floured surface, cut into four 5 in circles, and then trim into shell shapes. Brush with a little beaten egg and mark a shell pattern on each with a small knife. Place on a baking sheet, chill and rest for 1 hour. Preheat the oven to 400°F.

*2* Melt 2 tbsp of the butter in a pan, season the scallops and cook for not longer than 30 seconds over a high heat. Transfer to a plate.

*3* Bake the pastry shapes for 20–25 minutes until golden and dry. Sauté the shallots, celery and carrots gently in the remaining butter without coloring. Add the mushrooms and cook over a moderate heat until the juices begin to run. Pour in the vermouth and increase the heat to evaporate the juices.

*4* Add the crème fraîche and cooked scallops and bring to a simmer (do not boil). Remove the pan from the heat and blend in the egg yolks. Return the pan to a gentle heat and cook for a moment or two until the sauce has thickened to the consistency of thin cream, remove the pan from the heat. Season and add the lemon juice.

*5* Split the pastry shapes open and place on four plates. Spoon in the filling and replace the tops. Serve with potatoes and salad.

### Cook's Tip
Take care not to use dark mushrooms in a cream sauce.

## Clam, Mushroom and Potato Chowder

### SERVES 4

| |
|---|
| 48 medium clams, washed |
| 1 tbsp unsalted butter |
| 1 large onion, chopped |
| 1 celery stalk, sliced |
| 1 medium carrot, peeled and sliced |
| 8 oz / 2½ cups assorted wild mushrooms such as chanterelles, saffron milk-caps, chicken of the woods or oyster mushrooms, trimmed and sliced |
| 8 oz potatoes, peeled and thickly sliced |
| 5 cups light chicken or vegetable broth, boiling |
| 1 sprig thyme |
| 3 tbsp chopped fresh parsley, plus 4 parsley stalks |
| salt and freshly ground black pepper |

*1* Place the clams in a large stainless steel pan, put ½ in of water in the bottom, cover and steam over a moderate heat for 6–8 minutes.

*2* When open, drain the clams over a bowl, remove the shells and chop. Strain the juices over and set aside.

*3* Add the butter, onion, celery and carrot to the pan and soften without coloring. Add the mushrooms and cook for 3–4 minutes until their juices begin to run. Add the potatoes, the clams and their juices, the broth, thyme and parsley stalks. Bring to a boil and simmer for 25 minutes, or until the potatoes begin to fall apart. Season to taste, ladle into soup plates, sprinkle with parsley and serve.

### Cook's Tip
If clams are not available, use the same quantity of mussels.

## Snails with Ceps

### SERVES 4

| |
|---|
| 12 oz puff pastry, thawed if frozen |
| 1 egg, beaten, to glaze |
| ½ cup grated Parmesan |
| 4 tbsp unsalted butter |
| 2 shallots, finely chopped |
| 2 oz fennel, finely chopped |
| 2 oz fine green beans, cut in three |
| 4 oz / 1¼ cups fresh ceps, sliced, or ½ oz / ¼ cup dried ceps, soaked in warm water for 20 minutes and chopped |
| 1 garlic clove, crushed |
| 5 tbsp dry sherry |
| ⅔ cup beef broth, boiling |
| 2 tsp cornstarch |
| 1 tsp Dijon mustard |
| 2 × 7 oz cans snails, drained |
| ½ tsp black olive paste |
| 1 tsp balsamic or wine vinegar |
| salt and freshly ground black pepper |
| 3 tbsp chopped fresh parsley |

*3* Preheat the oven to 400°F. Melt the butter in a large nonstick frying pan, and gently fry the shallots, fennel and beans until soft but not brown. Add the ceps and garlic and sauté for another 6 minutes. Add the sherry and broth and simmer briefly. Bake the pastry shapes for 25 minutes until crisp.

*1* Roll out the pastry on a floured surface to a 12 in square. Cut out eight 4 in fluted rings, then cut four circles with a 3 in plain cutter. Place the four circles on a baking sheet, top each with two pastry rings and brush with beaten egg.

*2* Roll out the trimmings in a dusting of Parmesan cheese, cut into ¾ in wide strips and wind around four cream horn molds. Chill all the pastry shapes for about 1 hour.

*4* Place the cornstarch and the mustard in a cup and blend with 1 tbsp cold water. Stir the cornstarch mixture into the pan and simmer to thicken. Add the snails and the olive paste and simmer to heat through, then add the vinegar and season to taste.

*5* Spoon the mixture into the pastry shapes and sprinkle with chopped parsley. Serve with creamed potatoes and Savoy cabbage.

## Fillets of Trout with a Spinach and Field Mushroom Sauce

Many people like the idea of trout, but have trouble getting it off the bone. Trout fillets are the answer to this problem and taste delicious with a rich spinach and mushroom sauce.

### SERVES 4

4 brown or rainbow trout, filleted and skinned to make 8 fillets

**For the Spinach and Mushroom Sauce**

6 tbsp unsalted butter

¼ medium onion, chopped

8 oz / 2½ cups closed field or horse mushrooms, chopped

1¼ cups homemade or canned chicken broth, boiling

8 oz frozen chopped spinach

2 tsp cornstarch

⅔ cup crème fraîche

salt and freshly ground black pepper

grated nutmeg

*1* To make the sauce, melt 4 tbsp of the butter in a frying pan and sauté the onion until soft. Add the mushrooms and cook until the juices begin to run. Add the broth and the spinach and cook until the spinach has completely thawed.

*2* Blend the cornstarch with 1 tbsp of cold water and stir into the mushroom mixture. Simmer gently to thicken.

*3* Purée the sauce until smooth, add the crème fraîche and season to taste with salt and pepper and a pinch of nutmeg. Turn into a serving pitcher and keep warm.

*4* Melt the remaining butter in a large nonstick frying pan. Season the trout and cook for 6 minutes, turning once. Serve with new potatoes and young carrots with the sauce either poured over or served separately.

### Cook's Tip
Spinach and mushroom sauce is also good with fillets of cod, haddock and sole.

## Puff Pastry Salmon with Chanterelle Cream Filling

The flavor of farmed salmon is helped by a creamy layer of chanterelle mushrooms.

### SERVES 6

| |
|---|
| 12 oz puff pastry, thawed if frozen |
| 1 egg, beaten, to glaze |
| 2 large salmon fillets, about 2 lb total weight, skinned and boned |
| 1⅝ cups dry white wine |
| 1 small carrot |
| 1 small onion, halved |
| ½ celery stalk, chopped |
| 1 sprig thyme |
| **For the Chanterelle Cream** |
| 2 tbsp unsalted butter |
| 2 shallots, chopped |
| 8 oz / 2½ cups chanterelles or saffron milk-caps, trimmed and sliced |
| 5 tbsp white wine |
| ⅔ cup heavy cream |
| 3 tbsp chopped fresh chervil |
| 2 tbsp chopped fresh chives |
| **For the Hollandaise Sauce** |
| ¾ cup unsalted butter |
| 2 egg yolks |
| 2 tsp lemon juice |
| salt and freshly ground black pepper |

*1* Preheat the oven to 400°F. Roll out the pastry on a floured surface to form a rectangle 4 in longer and 2 in wider than the fillets. Trim into a fish shape, decorate with a pastry cutter and glaze with beaten egg. Chill for at least 1 hour and then bake for 30–35 minutes until puffed and golden. Remove from the oven, cool slightly, and split open horizontally. Reduce the oven temperature to 325 °F.

*2* To make the chanterelle cream, sauté the shallots gently in butter until soft but not colored. Add the mushrooms and cook until their juices begin to run. Pour in the wine, increase the heat and evaporate the juices. When dry, add the cream and herbs and bring to a simmer. Season well, transfer to a bowl, cover and keep warm.

*3* To poach the salmon fillets, place in a fish poacher or roasting pan. Add the wine, carrot, onion, celery, thyme and enough water to cover the fish. Bring to a boil slowly. As soon as the water begins to tremble, remove from the heat, cover and allow the fish to cook at this gentle simmer for 30 minutes.

*4* To make the sauce, melt the butter, skim the surface of any scum and pour into a small pitcher, leaving behind the milky residue. Place the yolks and 1 tbsp of water in a glass bowl and place over a pan of simmering water. Whisk the yolks until thick and foamy. Remove from the heat and very slowly pour in the butter, whisking all the time. Add the lemon juice and season.

*5* Place one salmon fillet on the base of the pastry, spread with the chanterelle cream and cover with the second fillet. Cover with the top of the pastry "fish" and warm through in the oven for about 10–15 minutes. Serve with the sauce.

### Cook's Tip

Fillets of cod or haddock would also be good in this pastry "fish".

## Wild Mushroom and Cep Cockle Puffs

This dish is as much a soup as it is a fish course. Oyster mushrooms, ceps and cockles or mussels combine in a rich herb broth and covered with pastry. When baked, the broth steams and the pastry puffs in a dome.

### SERVES 4

| |
|---|
| *12 oz puff pastry, thawed, if frozen* |
| *1 egg beaten, to glaze* |
| *3 tbsp sesame seeds or celery seed* |

### For the Soup

| |
|---|
| *2 tbsp unsalted butter* |
| *4 scallions, trimmed and chopped* |
| *1 celery stalk, sliced* |
| *1 small carrot, peeled, halved and sliced* |
| *4 oz / 1¼ cups fresh young ceps or bay boletes, sliced* |
| *6 oz / 1¾ cups oyster mushrooms* |
| *1⅞ cup whole milk* |
| *10 oz shelled fresh cockles or mussels, cooked* |
| *2 oz samphire or glasswort, trimmed (optional)* |
| *4 oz cooked potato, diced* |
| *4 sprigs thyme* |

*1* Roll out the pastry on a floured surface and cut into four 7 in rounds. Rest in a cool place for 1 hour. Preheat the oven to 375°F.

*2* Fry the scallions, celery and carrot in butter for 2–3 minutes. Add the mushrooms and sauté until the juices begin to flow. Transfer to a large saucepan.

*3* Pour the milk over the mushrooms and bring to a simmer. Add the cockles or mussels, samphire and potato.

*4* Heat through the contents of the saucepan and then ladle into four deep ovenproof soup bowls. Add a sprig of thyme to each.

*5* Moisten the edges of the bowls with beaten egg, cover with the pastry rounds and press the edges to seal. Brush with more beaten egg, sprinkle with sesame seeds and bake in the oven for 35–40 minutes until the pastry top is puffed and golden.

### Cook's Tip

Closed button or Cremini mushrooms can be substituted.

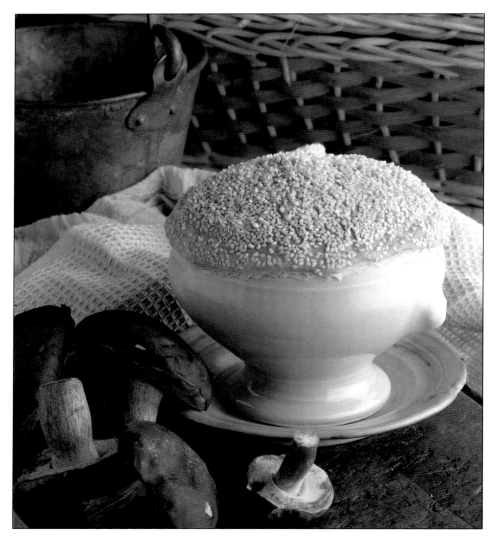

## Fresh Tuna Shiitake Teriyaki

Teriyaki is a sweet soy marinade usually used to glaze meat. Here Teri-yaki enhances fresh tuna steaks served with rich shiitake mushrooms.

### SERVES 4

| |
|---|
| 4 × 6oz fresh blue fin or yellow tail steaks |
| salt |
| ²/₃ cup Teriyaki sauce |
| 6 oz / 1¾ cups shiitake mushrooms, sliced |
| 8 oz white radish, peeled |
| 2 large carrots, peeled |

*1* Season the tuna steaks with a sprinkling of salt, then set aside for 20 minutes for it to penetrate. Pour the Teriyaki sauce over the fish and mushrooms and marinate for another 20–30 minutes or longer if you have the time.

**Cook's Tip**
A good Teriyaki sauce is made by Kikkoman and can be found in most large supermarkets.

*2* Preheat a moderate broiler or barbecue grill. Remove the tuna from marinade and reserve the marinade. Cook the tuna for 8 minutes, turning once.

*3* Transfer the mushrooms and marinade to a stainless steel saucepan and simmer for 3–4 minutes.

*4* Slice the radish and carrot thinly then shred finely with a chopping knife. Arrange in heaps on four serving plates and add the fish, with the mushrooms and sauce poured over. Serve with plain boiled rice.

## Turbans of Lemon Sole with a Paris Mushroom Twist

The Paris mushroom *champignon de Paris* or Cremini mushroom is the French equivalent of the English white button mushroom. Its mild woodland flavor goes well with the lemon sole.

**SERVES 4**

| |
| --- |
| *2 lb lemon sole, filleted and skinned to yield 1 lb of fish* |
| *5 tbsp dry white wine* |
| *½ cup water* |
| *3½ tbsp heavy cream* |
| *2 tsp cornstarch* |
| *2 tsp lemon juice* |
| *celery salt and cayenne pepper* |

**For the Mushroom Filling**

| |
| --- |
| *4 tbsp unsalted butter, plus extra for greasing* |
| *1 shallot, finely chopped* |
| *6 oz / 1¾ cups Cremini or oyster mushrooms, finely chopped* |
| *1 tbsp chopped fresh thyme* |
| *salt and freshly ground black pepper* |

*1* Preheat the oven to 375°F and butter an ovenproof casserole. Make the mushroom filling. Melt the butter in a frying pan and sauté the shallot until it is soft.

**Cook's Tip**
If planning ahead, the fish can be rolled and kept ready to cook for up to 8 hours.

*2* Add the mushrooms and thyme and cook until dry. Transfer to a bowl, season and allow to cool.

*3* Lay the fish skin side uppermost, season and spread with the filling. Roll up each fillet, then place in the buttered dish.

*4* Pour in the wine and water, then cover with a piece of buttered wax paper and cook in the oven for approximately 20 minutes.

*5* Transfer the fish to a warmed serving platter and strain the cooking juices into a small saucepan. Add the cream and bring to a simmer.

*6* Blend the cornstarch with 1 tbsp of water, add to the pan, stir and simmer to thicken, then add the lemon juice and season with celery salt and a pinch of cayenne pepper. Pour the sauce around the fish and serve with new potatoes, beans and carrots.

## Truffle and Lobster Risotto

To capture the precious qualities of the fresh truffle, partner it with lobster and serve in a silky smooth risotto. Both truffle shavings and truffle oil are added towards the end of cooking to preserve their flavor.

### SERVES 4

| |
|---|
| 4 tbsp unsalted butter |
| 1 medium onion, chopped |
| 2 cups Arborio or other short-grain rice |
| 1 sprig thyme |
| 5 cups chicken broth |
| 2/3 cup dry white wine |
| 1 freshly cooked lobster |
| 3 tbsp chopped fresh parsley and chervil |
| 3–4 drops truffle oil |
| 2 hard-boiled eggs, sliced |
| 1 fresh black or white truffle |

*1* Melt the butter in a large shallow pan, add the onion and fry gently until soft without letting it color. Add the rice and thyme and stir well to coat evenly with fat. Pour in the chicken broth and wine, stir once and cook uncovered for 15 minutes.

*2* Twist off the lobster tail, cut the underside with scissors and remove white tail meat. Slice half of the meat, then roughly chop the remainder. Break open the claws with a small hammer and remove the flesh, in one piece if possible.

**Cook's Tip**
To make the most of the aromatic truffle scent, keep the tuber in the rice jar for a few days. Alternatively store with the eggs at room temperature.

*3* Remove the rice from the heat, stir in the chopped lobster meat, herbs and truffle oil. Cover and let stand for 5 minutes.

*4* Divide among warmed dishes and arrange the lobster and hard-boiled egg slices and shavings of fresh truffle on top. Serve immediately.

## Creamy Fish and Mushroom Pie

Fish pie is a healthy and hearty dish for a hungry family. To help the fish go further, mushrooms provide both flavor and nourishment.

### SERVES 4

*8 oz / 2½ cups assorted wild and cultivated mushrooms such as oyster, button, chanterelle or chicken of the woods, trimmed and quartered*

*1½ lb cod or haddock fillet, skinned and diced*

*2½ cups milk, boiling*

### For the Topping

*2 lb floury potatoes, peeled and quartered*

*2 tbsp butter*

*⅔ cup milk*

*salt and freshly ground black pepper*

*grated nutmeg*

### For the Sauce

*4 tbsp unsalted butter*

*1 medium onion, chopped*

*½ celery stalk, chopped*

*½ cup all-purpose flour*

*2 tsp lemon juice*

*3 tbsp chopped fresh parsley*

**4** Slowly add the reserved liquid, stirring until absorbed. Return to the heat, stir and simmer to thicken. Add the lemon juice and parsley, season, then add to the baking pan.

**1** Preheat the oven to 400°F. Butter an ovenproof casserole, sprinkle the mushrooms over the bottom, add the fish and season with salt and pepper. Pour on the boiling milk, cover and cook in the oven for 20 minutes. Using a slotted spoon, transfer the fish and mushrooms to a 6¼ cup baking pan. Pour the poaching liquid into a small pitcher and set aside.

**2** Cover the potatoes with cold water, add a good pinch of salt and boil for 20 minutes. Drain and mash with the butter and milk. Season well.

**3** To make the sauce, melt the butter in a saucepan, add the onion and celery and fry until soft but not colored. Stir in the flour, then remove from the heat.

**5** Top with the mashed potato and return to the oven for 30–40 minutes until golden brown.

## Pan-fried Salmon with a Tarragon Mushroom Sauce

Tarragon has a distinctive aniseed flavour that is good with fish, cream and mushrooms. This recipe uses oyster mushrooms to provide both texture and flavor.

### SERVES 4

| |
|---|
| 4 tbsp unsalted butter |
| salt and cayenne pepper |
| 4 × 6 oz salmon steaks |
| 1 shallot, finely chopped |
| 6 oz / 1⅓ cups assorted wild and cultivated mushrooms such as oyster mushrooms, saffron milk-caps, bay boletes or cauliflower fungus, trimmed and sliced |
| ⅞ cup chicken or vegetable stock |
| 2 tsp cornstarch |
| ½ tsp mustard |
| 3½ tbsp sour cream |
| 3 tbsp chopped fresh tarragon |
| 1 tsp white wine vinegar |

**Cook's Tip**
Fresh tarragon will bruise and darken quickly after chopping, so prepare the herb as and when you need it.

_1_ Melt half of the butter in a large non-stick frying pan, season the salmon and cook over a moderate heat for 8 minutes, turning once. Transfer to a plate, cover and keep warm.

_2_ Heat the remaining butter in the pan and gently fry the shallot to soften without letting it color. Add the mushrooms and cook until the juices begin to flow. Add the stock and simmer for 2–3 minutes.

_3_ Put the cornstarch and mustard in a cup and blend with 1 tbsp of water. Stir into the mushroom mixture and bring to a simmer, stirring, to thicken. Add the cream, tarragon, vinegar and salt and cayenne pepper.

_4_ Spoon the mushrooms over each salmon steak and serve with new potatoes and a green salad.

## Fillets of Sole Bonne Femme

To capture the delicate flavor of flat fish, it is best cooked simply with wine and few good mushrooms.

**SERVES 4**

| |
| --- |
| ½ cup unsalted butter |
| 1 shallot, finely chopped |
| 5 oz / 1½ cups chanterelles, Cremini or button mushrooms, trimmed and sliced |
| 2 lb lemon sole, skinned and filleted to yield approximately 1 lb of fish |
| salt and cayenne pepper |
| 5 tbsp dry white wine |
| ⅞ cup homemade or canned fish or chicken broth |
| 1 tsp lemon juice |
| 2 lb potatoes, peeled, boiled and mashed |
| 1 tbsp chopped fresh Italian parsley, to garnish |

*1* Preheat the oven to 325°F. Sauté the shallot in 2 tbsp of the butter until soft. Turn into an ovenproof earthenware casserole and add the mushrooms. Place the fish fillets on top and season lightly.

*2* Pour in the wine and broth and cover with buttered wax paper. Cook in the oven for 25 minutes.

*3* Transfer to a flameproof serving dish and keep warm. Strain the liquid into a shallow frying pan, reserving the mushrooms and shallot. Boil the sauce rapidly until reduced to a syrupy liquid. Remove from the heat, add the remaining butter cut into small pieces and shake the pan (the sauce must not boil). Add the mushroom mixture, the lemon juice and seasoning.

*4* Heat the broiler to a moderate temperature. Pipe a border of potatoes around the dish, spoon the sauce over and heat under the broiler.

## Shrimp and Mushroom Kebabs

The flavor of grilled or barbecued shrimp combines especially well with chanterelles, chicken of the woods and saffron milk-caps. The mushrooms need to be blanched and then moistened with oil to prevent them from burning over the coals.

**SERVES 4**

| |
| --- |
| 6 oz / 1¾ cups wild mushrooms such as chanterelles, chicken of the woods, saffron milk caps, or shiitake, trimmed and cut into pieces |
| 3 tbsp olive oil |
| 12 large raw shrimp |
| 1 fennel bulb, thickly sliced |
| 8 cherry tomatoes |
| celery salt and cayenne pepper |

*1* Preheat a moderate broiler or barbecue. Bring a saucepan of water to a boil, and blanch the mushrooms for 30 seconds. Transfer to a bowl with a slotted spoon and add a little oil.

**Cook's Tip**
Buy fresh raw shrimp if you can, they taste much better than frozen.

*2* Moisten the shrimp with a little more oil, then thread onto four metal skewers alternating with the pieces of fennel, tomatoes and mushrooms.

*3* Season lightly, then broil for 6–8 minutes, turning once. Serve on a bed of long grain and wild rice with a simple green salad.

## Fruits of the Sea and Forest in Puff Pastry

The freshest fish and the finest wild mushrooms are combined here in a delicious cream sauce. The spectacular puff pastry shell is easier to make than it looks.

### SERVES 4

| |
|---|
| 12 oz puff pastry, thawed if frozen |
| 1 egg, beaten, to glaze |
| 7/8 cup dry white wine |
| 1 cup homemade or canned chicken or vegetable broth |
| 12 oz / 3½ cups assorted wild and cultivated mushrooms such as oyster, chanterelles, shiitake, hedgehog fungus, cauliflower fungus, saffron milk-caps, chicken of the woods or St George's mushrooms, trimmed and cut into thumb-sized pieces |
| 1 medium squid |
| 4 oz monkfish, boned and cut into large pieces |
| 12 mussels in their shells, scrubbed |
| 8 oz salmon fillet, skinned and cut into bite-sized pieces |
| 12 large raw shrimp, peeled |
| 6 sea scallops, halved |
| 4 tbsp unsalted butter |
| 2 shallots, finely chopped |
| 4 tbsp all-purpose flour |
| 5 tbsp crème fraîche |
| 2 tsp lemon juice |
| salt and cayenne pepper |

*1* Roll out the pastry on a floured surface to form a rectangle 12 × 15 in. Cut out a 9 in circle and place on a baking sheet. Prick all over with a fork and brush the surface with beaten egg. Cut out 1½ in circles with a fluted pastry cutter. Overlap these shapes around the edge of the large circle, brush again with egg and chill for 1 hour in a fridge. Preheat the oven to 400°F.

*2* Bring the wine and broth to a simmer, add the mushrooms and cook gently for 3–4 minutes. Remove with a slotted spoon and set aside in a large bowl.

*3* To prepare the squid, pull the head and tentacles away from the body, sever the tentacles and chop coarsely. Remove the quill from inside the body, pull off the side fins and set aside. Rinse the body piece under water and rub off the fine outer skin. Cut the body piece in half lengthways, open out and score a criss-cross pattern with a sharp knife over the inside surface. Cut the squid into wide strips.

*4* Tap the mussels sharply and discard any that do not close.

*5* Bring the wine and broth to a simmer and add the squid, monkfish, mussels, salmon, shrimp and scallops and cook for 6 minutes. Remove with a slotted spoon and add to the bowl with the mushrooms. Discard any mussels which have not opened. Strain the cooking liquid and make up to 1½ cups with water, if necessary. Bake the pastry for 25–30 minutes until golden.

*6* Melt the butter in a saucepan, add the shallots and fry gently until soft but not colored. Stir in the flour and remove from the heat. Gradually add the broth to make a smooth sauce and then return to the heat and simmer to thicken, stirring frequently.

*7* Add the crème fraîche and then stir in the mushrooms and fish. Add the lemon juice and season to taste. Spoon the mixture into the pastry shell and serve with buttered parsley potatoes and spring vegetables. There will be enough filling for an extra serving.

# Vegetarian Dishes

## Wild Mushroom Brioche with an Orange Butter Sauce

The finest wild mushrooms deserve the best treatment. Try this butter-rich brioche stuffed full of flavorsome fungi.

### SERVES 4

| |
|---|
| 1 tsp active dried yeast |
| 3 tbsp milk, at room temperature |
| 3½ cups white all-purpose flour |
| 1 tsp salt |
| 1 tbsp superfine sugar |
| 3 eggs |
| finely grated rind of ½ lemon |
| ⅞ cup unsalted butter, at room temperature |

**For the Filling**

| |
|---|
| 4 tbsp unsalted butter |
| 2 shallots, chopped |
| 12 oz / 3½ cups assorted wild and cultivated mushrooms, such as ceps, bay boletes, chanterelles, winter chanterelles, saffron milk-caps, oyster mushrooms and horn of plenty, trimmed, sliced and roughly chopped |
| ½ garlic clove, crushed |
| 5 tbsp chopped fresh parsley |
| salt and freshly ground black pepper |

**For the Orange Butter Sauce**

| |
|---|
| 2 tbsp frozen orange juice concentrate |
| ¾ cup unsalted butter, diced |
| salt and cayenne pepper |

**1** Dissolve the yeast in the milk, add 1 cup of the flour and mix to form a dough. Fill a bowl with warm water, then place the dough in the water. Leave for 30 minutes in a warm place to activate the yeast.

**2** Place the remaining 2½ cups of flour in the bowl of a food processor fitted with the dough or metal blade and add the salt, sugar, eggs, lemon rind and the risen dough and process briefly to mix. Add the diced butter and process until the dough is silky smooth and very elastic. Lift the dough out onto a sheet of plastic wrap and refrigerate for 2 hours until firm. Meanwhile, preheat the oven to 375°F.

**3** Sauté the shallots in the butter without letting them brown. Add the mushrooms and garlic, allow the juices to run and then increase the heat to reduce the moisture. When dry, turn into a bowl, add the parsley, season well and allow to cool.

**4** Grease and line a 2 lb loaf tin with non-stick wax paper. Roll the brioche out on a floured surface to form a rectangle 6 × 12 in. Spoon the cooked mushrooms over the dough and roll up to make a fat sausage. Drop the dough into the loaf pan, cover with a damp dish towel and leave to rise in a warm humid place for 50 minutes. When the dough has risen above the level of the rim, place in the oven and bake for 40 minutes.

**5** To make the sauce, place the orange juice concentrate in a heatproof glass bowl and heat by standing in a saucepan of simmering water. Remove the pan from the heat, and gradually whisk in the butter until creamy. Season to taste, cover and keep warm. When the brioche is cooked, turn it out, slice and serve with orange butter sauce and a simple green salad.

**Cook's Tip**
Allow plenty of time for this recipe. It helps to make the dough and filling ahead and chill them until needed.

## Mushroom Picker's Omelet

Enthusiastic mushroom pickers have been known to carry with them a portable gas stove, an omelet pan and a few eggs, ready to assemble an on-site brunch.

### SERVES 1

2 tbsp unsalted butter, plus extra for cooking

4 oz / 1¼ cups assorted wild and cultivated mushrooms such as young ceps, bay boletes, chanterelles, saffron milk-caps, closed field mushrooms, oyster mushrooms, hedgehog and matsatake mushrooms, trimmed and sliced

3 eggs, at room temperature

salt and freshly ground black pepper

*1* Melt the butter in a small omelet pan, add the mushrooms and cook until the juices run. Season, remove from pan and set aside. Wipe the pan.

*2* Break the eggs into a bowl, season and beat with a fork. Heat the omelet pan over a high heat, add a pat of butter and let it begin to brown. Pour in the beaten egg and stir briskly with the back of a fork.

*3* When the eggs are two-thirds scrambled, add the mushrooms and let the omelet finish cooking for 10–15 seconds.

**Cook's Tip**

From start to finish, an omelet should be cooked and on the table in less than a minute. For best results use farm fresh eggs at room temperature.

*4* Tap the handle of the omelet pan sharply with your fist to loosen the omelet from the pan, then fold and turn onto a plate. Serve with warm crusty bread and a simple green salad.

## Open Cap Mushrooms Stuffed with Hummus and Herbs

The up-turned cap of the field mushroom provides an ideal resting place for a spoonful of hummus; made here from canned chick-peas.

### SERVES 4

| |
| --- |
| 12 medium open cap field mushrooms |
| 4 tbsp olive oil |
| 2 tbsp lemon juice |
| **For the Hummus** |
| 14 oz can chick-peas, drained |
| 2 tbsp tahini |
| 2 garlic cloves, crushed |
| 5 tbsp olive oil |
| celery salt and cayenne pepper |
| 6 tbsp chopped fresh parsley |
| 2 tbsp mild paprika |
| stuffed olives, to garnish |

**Cook's Tip**
Tahini is a thick paste made from sesame seeds. It can be found in Middle Eastern food stores and most large supermarkets.

*1* Preheat the oven to 375°F. Meanwhile, snap off the mushroom stems at the base and save for use in another recipe.

*2* Combine the olive oil with 2 tsp lemon juice in a cup and liberally brush over the insides of the mushroom caps. Arrange on a baking sheet and cook in the oven for 25 minutes. Allow to cool.

*3* To make the hummus, blend the chick-peas in a food processor until smooth, add the tahini, garlic and olive oil. Process well, then season with celery salt and cayenne pepper.

*4* Spoon the hummus into the mushroom cups, then mold into cone shapes, mask one side with the chopped parsley and dust the other with mild paprika. Serve at room temperature garnished with the olives, with bread and pickled green peppers.

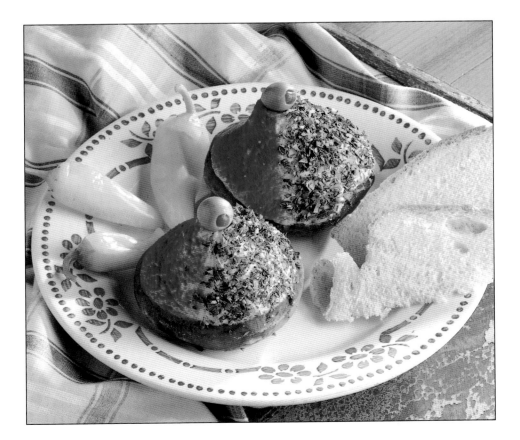

## Creamy Beet and Potato Gratin with Wild Mushrooms

Polish communities make the most of robust flavors in their cooking and are often first in the woods when mushrooms appear. This inexpensive dish captures the spirit of their autumn menus.

### SERVES 4

| 2 tbsp vegetable oil |
| 1 medium onion, chopped |
| 3 tbsp all-purpose flour |
| 1¼ cups vegetable broth |
| 1½ lb cooked beets, peeled and chopped |
| 5 tbsp light cream |
| 2 tbsp horseradish sauce |
| 1 tsp hot mustard |
| 1 tbsp wine vinegar |
| 1 tsp caraway seeds |
| 2 tbsp unsalted butter |
| 1 shallot, chopped |

8 oz / 2½ cups assorted wild and cultivated mushrooms such as ceps, bay boletes, chanterelles, chicken of the woods, blewits, fairy ring, parasol, oyster, field, shiitake, hen of the woods and honey mushrooms, trimmed and sliced

| 3 tbsp chopped fresh parsley |

**For the Potato Border**

| 2 lb floury potatoes, peeled |
| ⅔ cup milk |
| 1 tbsp chopped fresh dill (optional) |
| salt and freshly ground black pepper |

*1* Preheat the oven to 375°F. Lightly oil a 9 in round baking dish. Heat the oil in a large saucepan, add the onion and sauté until soft without coloring. Stir in the flour, remove from the heat and gradually add the broth, stirring until well blended.

*2* Return to the heat, stir and simmer to thicken, then add the beets, cream, horseradish, mustard, vinegar and caraway seeds.

*3* Bring the potatoes to a boil in salted water and cook for 20 minutes. Drain well and mash with the milk. Add the dill if using and season to taste with salt and pepper.

*4* Spoon the potatoes into the prepared dish and make a well in the center. Spoon the beet mixture into the well and set aside.

*5* Melt the butter in a large nonstick frying pan and sauté the shallot until soft, without browning. Add the mushrooms and cook over a moderate heat until their juices begin to run. Increase the heat and boil off the moisture. When dry, season and stir in the chopped parsley. Spread the mushrooms over the beet mixture, cover and bake for 30 minutes.

**Cook's Tip**
If planning ahead, this entire dish can be made in advance and heated through when needed. Allow 50 minutes baking time from room temperature.

## Chicken of the Woods Saté with a Spiced Hazelnut Sauce

To capture the texture and flavor of chicken of the woods, marinate them in a rich hazelnut sauce.

### SERVES 4

| |
| --- |
| *12 oz / 3½ cups chicken of the woods, trimmed and diced* |
| *½ cup hazelnuts, toasted* |
| *1 shallot, quartered* |
| *2 oz crustless white bread* |
| *2 tbsp hazelnut or olive oil* |
| *1⅞ cup boiling vegetable broth, homemade or canned* |
| *¼ tsp ground cinnamon* |
| *1 tsp honey* |
| *grated rind and juice of ½ small orange* |
| *½ tsp celery salt* |
| *¼ tsp cayenne pepper* |

*1* Cover the chicken of the woods with boiling water and leave for 2–3 minutes to soften. Thread onto bamboo skewers and set aside.

*2* Grind the hazelnuts in a food processor, add the shallot and process until smooth. Add the bread, oil, broth, cinnamon, honey, rind and juice. Blend again, then season to taste with celery salt and cayenne pepper.

*3* Spoon half of the marinade over the skewered chicken of the woods and set aside at room temperature for 30–40 minutes. Preheat a moderate broiler and cook for 8 minutes, turning once.

*4* Serve with couscous or rice, green salad and the remaining sauce, warm or at room temperature.

### Cook's Tip
Young chicken of the woods is best suited for this recipe. Older fungi tend to dry with age.

# Savoy Cabbage Stuffed with Mushroom Barley

The veined texture of savoy cabbage provides good cover for an earthy rich stuffing of barley and wild mushrooms.

### SERVES 4

4 tbsp unsalted butter

2 medium onions, chopped

1 celery stalk, sliced

8 oz / 2½ cups assorted wild and cultivated mushrooms such as young ceps, bay boletes, closed shaggy ink caps, chicken of the woods, saffron milk-caps, amethyst deceivers, oyster and closed field mushrooms, and blewits, trimmed, sliced and roughly chopped, or 2 tbsp dried ceps, bay boletes or saffron milk-caps, soaked in warm water for 20 minutes, and 7 oz / 2 cups Cremini mushrooms, roughly chopped

1¼ cups pearl barley

1 sprig fresh thyme

3⅔ cups water

2 tbsp almond or cashew nut butter

½ vegetable stock cube

salt and freshly ground black pepper

1 savoy cabbage

**Cook's Tip**
A range of nut butters is available in all leading health food stores.

*1* Melt the butter in a large heavy saucepan, add the onions and celery and sauté for 6–8 minutes until soft. Add the mushrooms and cook until they release their juices, then add the barley, thyme, water and the nut butter. Bring to a boil, cover and simmer for 30 minutes. Add the ½ stock cube and simmer for a further 20 minutes. Season to taste.

*2* Separate the cabbage leaves and cut away the thick stem. Blanch the leaves in salted boiling water for 3–4 minutes. Drain and refresh under cold running water. Drain again.

*3* Lay an 18in piece of cheesecloth over a steamer. Reconstruct the cabbage by lining the cheesecloth with large cabbage leaves. Spread a layer of mushroom barley over the leaves.

*4* Cover with a second layer of leaves and filling. Continue until the center is full. Draw together opposite corners of the cheesecloth and tie firmly. Place the cabbage in a steamer, set in a saucepan containing 1 in of simmering water, cover and steam for 30 minutes. To serve, place on a warmed serving plate, untie the cheesecloth and carefully pull it out from underneath the cabbage.

**Cook's Tip**
If planning ahead, the cabbage can be assembled well in advance before the final cooking. To ensure richness and flavor use a good portion of ceps, chicken of the woods and field mushrooms.

## Mushroom Picker's Pâté

A good vegetarian pâté should be as smooth and as rich as one made with fine liver. This recipe compares very favorably to traditional meat ones.

### SERVES 4

| |
|---|
| 3 tbsp vegetable oil |
| 1 medium onion, chopped |
| ½ celery stick, chopped |
| 12 oz / 3½ cups assorted wild and cultivated mushrooms such as closed field mushrooms, fairy ring, oyster and shiitake mushrooms, bay bolete and horn of plenty, trimmed and sliced |
| ⅔ cup red lentils |
| 2¼ cups homemade or canned vegetable broth or water |
| 1 sprig thyme |
| 4 tbsp almond or cashew nut butter |
| 1 garlic clove, crushed |
| 1 oz bread, crusts removed |
| 5 tbsp milk |
| 1 tbsp lemon juice |
| 4 egg yolks |
| celery salt and freshly ground black pepper |

*1* Preheat the oven to 350°F. Heat the oil in a large saucepan, add the onion and celery and brown lightly. Add the mushrooms and sauté for 3–4 minutes. Remove a spoonful of the mushroom pieces and set aside until they are needed.

*2* Add the lentils, stock and thyme, bring to a boil uncovered and simmer for 20 minutes or until the lentils have fallen apart.

*3* Place the nut butter, garlic, bread and milk in a food processor and blend until smooth.

*4* Add the lemon juice and egg yolks and combine. Add the lentil mixture, blend, then season well. Lastly stir the reserved mushrooms into the mixture.

*5* Turn the mixture into a 5 cup pâté or loaf pan, stand in a roasting pan half filled with boiling water, cover and cook for 50 minutes. Allow to cool before serving from the pan.

### Cook's Tip

If you are using only cultivated mushrooms, an addition of ⅓ oz / 3 tbsp of dried ceps, bay boletes, chanterelles and horn of plenty will provide a good wild mushroom flavor. Soak first in warm water for 20 minutes.

Almond or cashew nut butter is available from most good health food shops.

## Japanese Mushrooms with Lemon and Walnut Noodles

The flavor of the Japanese enokitaki mushroom is as fine as its appearance. This preparation captures their sweet peppery taste. If quail eggs are unobtainable, substitute the smallest chicken eggs.

### SERVES 4

| |
|---|
| ⅓ cup somen noodles or vermicelli pasta |
| 1 large carrot, peeled, sliced and shredded |
| 2¼ cups dashi, or light vegetable broth, made with a cube |
| ½ oz arame or hijiki dried seaweed |
| 2 oz / ¾ cup enokitaki mushrooms |
| 1 tsp lemon juice |
| 2 tsp walnut oil |
| 1 scallion, green part only, sliced |

*1* Cook the noodles and carrots in salted boiling water for 3–4 minutes. Drain, cool under running water and set aside.

### Cook's Tip

The enokitaki mushroom is a cultivated variety and is available from Japanese supermarkets worldwide. Dried seaweed and somen noodles can be found in most health food stores.

*2* Bring the dashi or stock to the boil, add the arame or seaweed and simmer for 2 minutes. Add the noodles, mushrooms, lemon juice and oil and briefly reheat.

*3* Divide among four Japanese soup bowls, sprinkle with scallion slices and serve.

## Late Summer Mushrooms and Vegetables in a Hazelnut Dressing

Seasonal flavors merge well with autumn mushrooms to give this vegetable dish distinctive character.

### SERVES 4

| |
|---|
| 2 tbsp vegetable oil |
| 1 shallot, chopped |
| 1 celery stalk, sliced |
| 8 oz / 2½ cups assorted wild and cultivated mushrooms such as young ceps, bay boletes, chanterelles, amethyst deceivers, horn of plenty, oyster, shiitake, queen boletes, Caesar's mushrooms and honey mushrooms, trimmed, sliced or halved if small |
| salt and freshly ground black pepper |
| 6 oz small potatoes, scrubbed or scraped |
| 1 cup young green beans, trimmed and halved |
| 4 oz baby carrots, trimmed and peeled |
| 1 cup fava beans |
| 3 tbsp hazelnut oil |
| 1 tbsp peanut oil |
| 1 tbsp lemon juice |
| 1 tsp chopped fresh thyme |
| 2 oz hazelnuts, toasted and chopped |

*1* Sauté the shallot and celery in vegetable oil until soft but without coloring. Add the mushrooms and cook over a moderate heat until their juices begin to run, then increase the heat to boil off the juices. Season and set aside.

*2* In separate pans, boil the potatoes for 20 minutes, beans and carrots for 6 minutes and the fava beans for 3 minutes. Drain and cool under running water, then remove the tough outer skins of the fava beans.

*3* Combine the vegetables with the mushrooms, then moisten with hazelnut and peanut oil. Add the lemon juice and thyme, season and sprinkle with toasted hazelnuts.

# Wild Mushroom Gratin with Fontina Cheese, New Potatoes, Pickles and Walnuts

This gratin is one of the simplest and most delicious ways of cooking mushrooms. The dish is inspired by the Swiss custom of eating alpine cheeses with new potatoes and small cornichons.

### SERVES 4

*2 lb new potatoes, scrubbed or scraped*

*4 tbsp unsalted butter or 4 tbsp olive oil*

*12 oz / 3½ cups assorted wild and cultivated mushrooms such as oyster, shiitake and closed field mushrooms, ceps, bay boletes, chanterelles, winter chanterelles, hedgehog fungus, matsutake mushrooms and saffron milk-caps*

*salt and freshly ground black pepper*

*6 oz Fontina cheese*

*½ cup walnut or pecan pieces, toasted*

*12 medium cornichons and mixed green salad leaves, to serve*

*1* Place the potatoes in a pan of salted water, bring to a boil and cook for 20 minutes. Drain, add the pat of butter, cover and keep warm.

*2* Trim the mushrooms and then slice them thinly.

*3* Sauté the mushrooms in the remaining butter or oil. When the juices appear, increase the heat to evaporate the moisture.

*4* Preheat a moderate broiler. Slice the cheese thinly, arrange on top of the mushroom slices and broil until bubbly and brown. Sprinkle with walnuts and serve with buttered new potatoes, cornichons and a green salad.

**Cook's Tip**
For best results, choose an attractive flameproof dish that can be put under the broiler and brought directly to the table.

## Hash Brown Chicken of the Woods with Potatoes and Onions

This hash brown dinner is a very special treat. It calls for the intriguing *Laetiporus sulphureus*, or chicken of the woods, which looks, tastes and has the texture of chicken, and that undefinable extra of wild mushroom.

### SERVES 4

| |
|---|
| 2 lb potatoes, peeled |
| 4 tbsp unsalted butter |
| 2 medium onions, sliced |
| 1 celery stalk, sliced |
| 1 small carrot, peeled and cut into small slices |
| 8 oz chicken of the woods, trimmed and sliced |
| 3 tbsp medium sherry |
| 3 tbsp chopped fresh parsley |
| 1 tbsp chopped fresh chives |
| grated rind of ½ lemon |
| salt and freshly ground black pepper |

*1* Place the potatoes in a saucepan of salted water, bring to a boil and cook for 20 minutes. Drain, cool and slice thickly.

**Cook's Tip**
The best hash browns are made from late season floury potatoes that are inclined to fall apart when cooked. This quality helps the mixture to form a more solid mass in the pan.

*2* Melt the butter in a large nonstick frying pan, add the onions, celery and carrot and sauté until lightly browned.

*3* Add the chicken of the woods and the sherry, then simmer to evaporate any moisture.

*4* Add the potatoes, herbs, lemon rind and seasoning, toss and fry together until crispy brown. Serve with a salad of frisée and young spinach leaves.

## Mushroom Börek

The Turkish *börek* is a rich pastry package with various savory fillings, such as the following.

### SERVES 4

| |
|---|
| 1/3 cup couscous |
| 3 tbsp olive oil |
| 1 medium onion, chopped |
| 8 oz / 2½ cups assorted wild and cultivated mushrooms such as ceps, bay boletes, chanterelles, winter chanterelles, oyster, field and Caesar's mushrooms, trimmed and sliced |
| 1 garlic clove, crushed |
| 4 tbsp chopped fresh parsley |
| 1 tsp chopped fresh thyme |
| 1 egg, hard-boiled and peeled |
| salt and freshly ground black pepper |

### For the Börek Pastry

| |
|---|
| 3½ cups self-rising flour |
| 1 tsp salt |
| 1 egg, plus extra for glazing |
| 2/3 cup plain yogurt |
| 2/3 cup olive oil |
| grated rind of ½ lemon |

### For the Yogurt Sauce

| |
|---|
| 7/8 cup plain yogurt |
| 3 tbsp chopped fresh mint |
| ½ tsp superfine sugar |
| ¼ tsp cayenne pepper |
| ¼ tsp celery salt |
| a little milk or water |

*1* Preheat the oven to 375°F. Just cover the couscous with boiling water and soak for 10 minutes or until the liquid is absorbed. Then sauté the onion in oil without letting it color. Add the mushrooms and garlic and cook until the juices begin to run, then increase the heat to evaporate the juices. Transfer to a bowl, add the parsley, thyme and couscous and stir well. Chop the hard-boiled egg into the mixture, season and combine.

*2* To make the pastry, sift the flour and salt into a bowl. Make a well, add the egg, yogurt, olive oil and lemon rind and combine with a fork.

*3* Turn out onto a floured surface and roll into a 12 in circle. Pile the mixture into the center of the pastry, and bring the edges over, to enclose the filling. Turn upside down onto a baking sheet. Press the börek out flat with your hand, glaze with beaten egg and bake for 25 minutes.

*4* To make the sauce, blend the yogurt with the mint, sugar, cayenne pepper and celery salt, adjusting the consistency with milk or water. Serve börek at room temperature.

## Egg and Rice Cakes with Sour Cream and Mushrooms

### SERVES 4

| |
|---|
| 1 egg |
| 1 tbsp all-purpose flour |
| 4 tbsp freshly grated Parmesan, Fontina or Pecorino cheese |
| 2 cups cooked long grain rice |
| salt and freshly ground black pepper |
| 4 tbsp unsalted butter, plus extra for frying |
| 1 shallot or small onion, chopped |
| 6 oz / 1¾ cups assorted wild and cultivated mushrooms such as ceps, bay boletes, chanterelles, winter chanterelles, horn of plenty, blewits, field and oyster mushrooms, trimmed and sliced |
| 1 sprig thyme |
| 2 tbsp Madeira or sherry |
| 2/3 cup sour cream or crème fraîche |
| paprika for dusting (optional) |

*1* Beat the egg, flour and cheese together with a fork, then stir in the cooked rice. Mix well and set aside.

*2* Sauté the shallot or onion in half the butter until soft but not brown. Add the mushrooms and thyme and cook until the juices run. Add the Madeira or sherry. Increase the heat to reduce the juices and concentrate the flavor. Season to taste, transfer to a bowl, cover and keep warm.

*3* Fry spoonsful of the rice mixture in a pat of butter. Cook each one for a minute on each side. When all the rice cakes are cooked, arrange on four warmed plates, top with sour cream or crème fraîche and a spoonful of mushrooms. Dust with paprika and serve with asparagus and baby carrots.

## Pumpkin Gnocchi with a Chanterelle Parsley Cream

Gnocchi is an Italian pasta dumpling usually made from potatoes, in this special recipe, pumpkin is added, too. A chanterelle sauce provides both richness and flavor.

### SERVES 4

| |
|---|
| *1 lb peeled floury potatoes* |
| *1 lb peeled pumpkin, chopped* |
| *2 egg yolks* |
| *1¾ cups all-purpose flour, plus more if necessary* |
| *pinch of ground allspice* |
| *¼ tsp ground cinnamon* |
| *pinch of grated nutmeg* |
| *finely grated rind of ½ orange* |
| *salt and freshly ground pepper* |

**For the Sauce**

| |
|---|
| *2 tbsp olive oil* |
| *1 shallot* |
| *6 oz / 2 cups fresh chanterelles, sliced, or ½ oz / ¼ cup dried, soaked for 20 minutes in warm water* |
| *2 tsp almond butter* |
| *⅔ cup crème fraîche* |
| *a little milk or water* |
| *5 tbsp chopped fresh parsley* |
| *½ cup grated Parmesan or Romano cheese* |

### Cook's Tip

If planning ahead, gnocchi can be shaped ready for cooking up to 8 hours in advance. Almond butter is available ready-made from health food shops.

*1* Cover the potatoes with cold salted water, bring to a boil and cook for 20 minutes. Drain and set aside. Place the pumpkin in a bowl, cover and microwave on full power for 8 minutes. Alternatively, wrap the pumpkin in foil and bake at 350°F for 30 minutes. Drain well, then add to the potato and pass through a vegetable mill into a bowl. Add the egg yolks, flour, spices, orange rind and seasoning and mix well to make a soft dough. Add more flour if the mixture is too loose.

*2* Bring a large pan of salted water to the boil, then lightly cover a work surface with all-purpose flour. Spoon the gnocchi mixture into an icing bag fitted with a ½ in plain nozzle. Pipe onto the floured surface to make a 6 in sausage. Roll in flour and cut into 1 in pieces. Repeat the process making more sausage shapes. Mark each lightly with a fork and cook for 3–4 minutes in the boiling water.

*3* Meanwhile, make the sauce. Heat the oil in a nonstick frying pan, add the shallot and fry until soft without coloring. Add the chanterelles and cook briefly, then add the almond butter. Stir to melt and stir in the crème fraîche. Simmer briefly and adjust the consistency with milk or water. Add the parsley and season to taste.

*4* Lift the gnocchi out of the water with a slotted spoon, turn into bowls and spoon the sauce over the top. Sprinkle with Parmesan cheese.

## Goat Cheese Kasha with Ceps and Walnuts

Kasha is a Russian staple of cooked grains. Robustly flavored buckwheat is most common and is often combined with other grains. Couscous is used here and allows the flavor of buckwheat, goat cheese, dried ceps and toasted walnuts to come through.

### SERVES 4

| |
|---|
| 1 cup couscous |
| 3 tbsp buckwheat |
| 1/4 cup dried ceps or bay boletes |
| 3 eggs |
| 4 tbsp chopped fresh parsley |
| 2 tsp chopped fresh thyme |
| 4 tbsp olive oil |
| 3 tbsp walnut oil |
| 1 1/2 cups crumbly white goat cheese |
| 1/2 cup walnut pieces, toasted |
| salt and freshly ground black pepper |
| salad and rye bread, to serve |

**Cook's Tip**
The flavor of buckwheat may be too strong for some tastes. In this case replace with couscous. Kasha can also be made from bulgur wheat or millet.

*1* Place the couscous, buckwheat and ceps in a bowl, cover with boiling water and let soak for 15 minutes. Drain off any excess liquid.

*2* Place the mixture in a large nonstick frying pan, add the eggs, season well, then scramble with a flat wooden spoon over a moderate heat.

*3* Stir in the parsley, thyme, olive oil, walnut oil, goat cheese and walnuts. Season to taste with salt and pepper.

*4* Transfer to a large serving dish and serve hot with rye bread, salad and Eastern European beer if available.

# GLOSSARY

**asci** The sacs in Ascomycetes in which the sexual spores are formed.

**Acomycetes** Group of fungi characterized by bearing the sexual spores in a sac (asci).

**Basidiomycetes** Group of fungi characterized by the presence of spore-bearing cells called basidia.

**brackets** Shelf-like fruit bodies.

**cap** The portion of the mushroom bearing the gills and the tubes.

**convex** A surface that is curved or rounded outwards.

**decurrent** Running down the stem.

**fibrous** Composed of fine fibers or threads.

**flesh** Inner tubes of a fungus.

**fruit body** Structure on which the spore-producing cells are held.

**hymenium** Layer of spore-producing cells.

**inrolled** Curled inwards and down.

**marginate** With a distinct ridge or gutter-like margin.

**milk** Sticky fluid released by some fungi when damaged.

**network** A mesh or pattern of criss-crossed fine ridges.

**partial veil** The fine web of tissue connecting the cap margin to the stem.

**pores** The openings of the clustered tubes in Boletes and Polypores.

**recurved** Curving backwards, i.e. scales with recurved tips.

**ring** Remains of the partial veil left on the stem.

**scales** Small to large raised flakes or flaps of tissue, usually on the cap or stem surface.

**spore** Reproductive cell of typical mushroom.

**spore print** A thick deposit of spores dropped by a mushroom cap onto paper.

**stem** The 'stalk' on which a mushroom cap is raised up.

**striated** With distinct parallel grooves or lines especially at the cap edge.

**tubes** The downward pointing clusters of tubes on Boletes and Polypores within which the spores are produced.

**universal veil** The fine to thick covering of tissue which envelopes some fungi when immature.

**volva** Example of thick universal veil which remains as a sac at the base of the stem.

**OPPOSITE** *Horn of plenty*, Craterellus cornucopioides.

**LEFT** *Saffron milk-caps*, Lactarius deliciosus.

*Numbers in bold indicate the main entry.*

Amanitas, 34, 98

# INDEX TO RECIPES

# ADDRESSES OF MYCOLOGICAL SOCIETIES

**North American Mycological Association**
Kenneth Cochran, Executive
Secretary, NAMA
3556 Oakwood
Ann Arbor, MI 48104–5213
313–971–2552
E-mail: Internet:
KWCEE@UMICH.edu

**COMA**
**Connecticut Mycological Association**
c/o Sheine
930 Old Mill River Road
Pound Ridge, NY 10576–1833

**Illinois Mycological Association**
13535 Longview Drive
Lockport, IL 60441–9440

**Boston Mycological Club**
Karen Davis, Corresponding
Secretary
470 Washington St.
Holliston MA 01746

**Cercle des Mycologues de Montreal**
4101 rue Sherbrooke
Montreal PQ Canada – 2B2

**Puget Sound Mycological Society**
University of Washington
Urban Horticulture #GF–15
Seattle, WA 98195–0001

**Mycological Society of San Francisco**
P.O. Box 882163
San Francisco, CA 94188–2163

**Texas Mycological Society**
7445 Dillon Street
Houston, Texas 77061–2721

**BELOW** *Horn of plenty,* Craterellus cornucopioides.

# BIBLIOGRAPHY

ARORA, DAVID, *Mushrooms Demystified* 2nd ed., 10 Speed Press 1986.

BESSETTE, ALAN AND WALTER J. SUNDBERG, *Mushrooms: A Quick Reference Guide to Mushrooms of North America,* Field Guide Series, Collier Books, Macmillan 1987.

DICKENSON, COLIN and LUCAS, JOHN, ed., *The Encyclopedia of Mushrooms* Putnam 1979.

LINCOFF, GARY H., *The Audubon Society Field Guide of North American Mushrooms,* Chanticleer Press, Dutton 1978.

LINCOFF, GARY H., and GIOVANNI PARIONI, ed., *Simon and Schuster's Guide to Mushrooms,* Simon and Schuster 1981.

MILLER, ORSON K. JR., *Mushrooms of North America,* Chanticleer Press, Dutton 1978.

PHILLIPS, ROGER, *Mushrooms and North America: The Most Complete Guide Ever,* Little Brown 1991.

SMITH, ALEXANDER and NANCY S. WEBER, *Mushroom Hunter's Field Guide,* University of Michigan Press 1980

*nb.* There are now some excellent regional mushroom guides. If you don't have a university or a mycological society nearby, go to your local library or bookstore and check the *Subject* volume to *Books in Print.* In 1994 there were listed many such guides to the different regions of North America. They are very useful additions to the general guides.

# Acknowledgements

The publishers and authors would like to thank the following people for their help in the production of this book: Geoffrey Kibby of the International Institute of Entomology, London; Andrew Broderick of the Australian Wild Fungi Research Group, School of Horticulture, University of Western Sydney, Hawkesbury, Bourke Street, Richmond NSW 2753 Australia; Clive Houlder, mushroom hunter and supplier of specialist fungi; L'aquila Products, 40 Caledonian Road, London, for providing the truffles; Valerie Jordan and Avril Henley for their help in typing the manuscript; Mycologue, 35 King Henry's Road, London, for providing the knives; Patricia Michelson, La Fromagerie, 30 Highbury Park, London N5 2AA, specialist food finder; Taste of the Wild, 65 Overstrand Mansions, Prince of Wales Drive, London SW11 4EX, suppliers of wild mushrooms.

## Picture credits

*t = top, b = bottom, l = left, r = right*

Heather Angel page 103br
Timothy J. Baroni 111t, 111b
George Dickson 45t, 45b, 118
Geoffrey Kibby 67tl, 70t, 83, 81tl
George McCarthy 2, 6/7, 15b, 17t, 22/23, 24, 28l, 28r, 29b, 34, 35b, 47b, 59t, 59b, 61t, 63m, 65b, 73t, 77b, 82tr, 82r, 96/97, 98, 106, 107l, 107r, 113b, 246
Gregory Mueller 31b, 61b, 63b, 66/67, 81b, 82l, 93, 115
Oxford Scientific Films (David Thompson) 29t; (G I Bernard) 30, 31t; (Jack Dermid) 105t

**BELOW** *Winter chanterelle,* Cantharellus infundibuliformis.

256